THE
THANKSGIVING PLAY

WHAT WOULD
CRAZY HORSE DO?

THE
THANKSGIVING PLAY

WHAT WOULD
CRAZY HORSE DO?

Larissa FastHorse

THEATRE COMMUNICATIONS GROUP / NEW YORK / 2021

The publication of *The Thanksgiving Play / What Would Crazy Horse Do?* by Larissa FastHorse, through TCG's Book Program, is made possible in part by the New York State Council on the Arts with the support of Governor Andrew Cuomo and the New York State Legislature.

Special thanks to Stephanie Ansin and Spencer Stewart for their generous support of this publication.

TCG books are exclusively distributed to the book trade by Consortium Book Sales and Distribution.

Library of Congress Control Numbers:
2021013473 (print) / 2021013474 (ebook)
ISBN 978-1-55936-961-9 (paperback) / ISBN 978-1-55936-925-1 (ebook)
A catalog record for this book is available from the Library of Congress.

Cover, book design and composition by Lisa Govan
Cover photo by Conor Horgan

First Edition, May 2021
Third Printing, January 2024

There are too many theaters and organizations around the United States to name who had a part in shaping these plays and my voice as a playwright. But I am deeply grateful to every member of our national theater community for their support.

The one name I must always list is Edd Hogan. He is my partner in all things. He told me to write plays when I thought I couldn't. He told me to do comedy when everyone asked for drama. He is my anchor so I can fly. Thank you, my love. We did it.

CONTENTS

THE
THANKSGIVING PLAY

The Thanksgiving Play was commissioned and produced by Artists Repertory Theatre (Dámaso Rodríguez, Artistic Director; J. S. May, Managing Director) in Portland, Oregon, on April 7, 2018. It was directed by Luan Schooler. The scenic design was by Megan Wilkerson, the costume design was by Emily Horton, the lighting design was by Kristeen Willis, the sound design and original music were by Ed Littlefield; the production stage manager was Carol Ann Wohlmut. The cast was:

LOGAN	Sarah Lucht
JAXTON	Michael O'Connell
ALICIA	Claire Rigsby
CADEN	Chris Harder

The Thanksgiving Play received its world premiere at Playwrights Horizons (Tim Sanford, Artistic Director; Leslie Marcus, Managing Director) in New York City, on October 12, 2018. It was directed by Moritz von Stuelpnagel. The scenic design was by Wilson Chin, the costume and puppet design were by Tilly Grimes, the lighting design was by Isabella Byrd, the sound design was by Mikaal Sulaiman; the production stage manager was Katie Ailinger. The cast was:

LOGAN	Jennifer Bareilles
JAXTON	Greg Keller
ALICIA	Margo Seibert
CADEN	Jeffrey Bean

The Thanksgiving Play was produced by Geffen Playhouse (Matt Shakman, Artistic Director; Gil Cates, Jr., Executive Director) in Los Angeles, on October 26, 2019. It was directed by Michael John Garcés. The scenic design was by Sara Ryung Clement, the costume design was by Garry Lennon, the lighting design was by Tom Ontiveros, the sound design was by Cricket S. Myers; the production stage manager was Samantha Cotton. The cast was:

LOGAN	Samantha Sloyan
JAXTON	Noah Bean
ALICIA	Alexandra Henrikson
CADEN	Jeff Marlow

CHARACTERS

LOGAN: Female, Caucasian-looking, the high school drama teacher who's always pushing the envelope in potentially inappropriate ways. Earnest about theater and proving herself.

JAXTON: Male, Caucasian-looking, yoga practitioner/actor. Politically correct to a fault, a big one. He's that confident guy everyone loves, but his logical PC-thinking takes weird turns.

ALICIA: Female, brunette, Caucasian-looking, but has looks that would have been cast as ethnic in 1950s movies. Without guile. Sexy and hot, but not bright.

CADEN: Male, Caucasian-looking, the academic. Awkward elementary school history teacher with dramatic aspirations but no experience.

NOTE

Scenes One, Three, Five, and Seven are sadly inspired by the internet, mostly current teachers' Pinterest boards. Play with the theatricality of these scenes; perhaps children perform them, perhaps puppets, perhaps the actors as children, perhaps video, perhaps anything. Have fun.

"ALL" means to play with who says what, *not* that everyone says it together.

Setting for the rest of the scenes is a high school drama room anywhere but the Los Angeles area.

MORE INFO

There have been a lot of productions of *The Thanksgiving Play*. For scenes and photos and links:

#thethanksgivingplay

SCENE ONE

Performers enter in school Thanksgiving outfits: Pilgrims, etc. They sing to the tune of "The Twelve Days of Christmas." Solos and movement encouraged.

ACTOR: www.childhood101.com/preschoolcountingsongs.

ALL:
> On the first day of Thanksgiving
> The Natives gave to me
> A pumpkin in a pumpkin patch.
>
> On the second day of Thanksgiving
> The Natives gave to me
> Two turkey gobblers,
> And a pumpkin in a pumpkin patch.
>
> On the third day of Thanksgiving
> The Natives gave to me

Three Native headdresses,
Two turkey gobblers,
And a pumpkin in a pumpkin patch.

On the fourth day of Thanksgiving,
The Natives gave to me
Four bows and arrows,
Three Native headdresses,
Two turkey gobblers,
And a pumpkin in a pumpkin patch.

On the fifth day of Thanksgiving,
The Natives gave to me
Five pairs of moccasins,
Four bows and arrows,
Three Native headdresses,
Two turkey gobblers,
And a pumpkin in a pumpkin patch.

On the sixth day of Thanksgiving,
The Natives gave to me
Six Native teepees,
Five pairs of moccasins,
Four bows and arrows,
Three Native headdresses,
Two turkey gobblers,
And a pumpkin in a pumpkin patch.

On the seventh day of Thanksgiving,
The Natives gave to me
Seven Native tom-toms,
Six Native teepees,
Five pairs of moccasins,
Four bows and arrows,

Three Native headdresses,
Two turkey gobblers,
And a pumpkin in a pumpkin patch.

On the eighth day of Thanksgiving,
The Natives gave to me
Eight woven blankets,
Seven Native tom-toms,
Six Native teepees,
Five pairs of moccasins,
Four bows and arrows,
Three Native headdresses,
Two turkey gobblers,
And a pumpkin in a pumpkin patch.

On the ninth day of Thanksgiving,
The Natives gave to me
Nine cornucopias,
Eight woven blankets,
Seven Native tom-toms,
Six Native teepees,
Five pairs of moccasins,
Four bows and arrows,
Three Native headdresses,
Two turkey gobblers,
And a pumpkin in a pumpkin patch.

ACTOR: Teacher's note: This song can do more than teach counting. I divide my students into Indians and Pilgrims, so the Indians can practice sharing.

SCENE TWO

A high school drama department classroom. It's bright and open with large recycle bins and a trendy water dispenser (alkaline, deionized, sewer, whatever is hippest). The walls are lined with cast photos, Shakespeare pun posters, and funny props. The usual high school play posters are represented along with some surprising ones like The Shipment, Extremities, The Iceman Cometh.

Jaxton and Logan's clothes come from overpriced vintage/hip clothing stores where clothes from ten years ago are considered "retro." Alicia shops at Urban Outfitters with deliberate touches of money: Prada sunglasses, the "it" jeans of the moment, etc. Caden shops at the Gap, Banana Republic for something dressy. He carries a briefcase of papers.

Jaxton is purposefully never organized; he's on the floor, draped backward over a chair. Logan and Caden are institutionalized; they sit forward in chairs, although Logan fights it. All of them fall into yoga asanas from time to time, although Caden's aren't as skillful.

Occasional "snaps" from everyone.

Jaxton and Logan set up the food table. Logan discovers a small cotton bag.

LOGAN: Is this for me?

JAXTON: Happy first day of rehearsal.

LOGAN: Jaxton, you didn't have to get me anything.

JAXTON: I know this gig is important to you so I want you to have something extra special.

(She opens the bag excitedly and pulls out . . . a mason jar.)

LOGAN: Oh. Wow. It's great.

JAXTON: It's a water bottle.

LOGAN: Sure.

JAXTON: It's made with recycled glass from broken windows in housing projects.

LOGAN: No way? That's amazing!

JAXTON: I know.

LOGAN: Where did you find it?

JAXTON: At the farmers market. It's symbolic of the way we're going to create this play. We start with this pile of jagged facts and misguided governmental policies and historical stereotypes about race then turn all that into something beautiful and dramatic and educational for the kids.

LOGAN: It's perfect. Thanks for getting me this gig. I'm not going to screw it up.

(They hug.
Jaxon pulls out a wedge of cheese.)

What's that?

JAXTON: What's what?

LOGAN: Is that soy cheese or coagulated cheese squeezed from a cow?

JAXTON: Coagulated.

11

You know I'm a vegan ally, but I've come to realize that I like cheese on my crackers.

LOGAN: I already struggle with the holiday of death.

JAXTON: If you're planning on "The Holiday of Death" as the title of our Thanksgiving play you'll lose your job for sure.

LOGAN: This is far more than a Thanksgiving play now. I got the Gender Equity in History Grant, the Excellence in Educational Theater Fellowship, a municipal arts grant and the Go! Girls! Scholastic Leadership Mentorship.

JAXTON: I know parents, to get them back on your side, you need to kill a turkey.

LOGAN: I'm a vegan.

JAXTON: You're a teaching artist with a three hundred parent petition to fire you.

LOGAN: I am staying in the positive. This kind of talk isn't helping.

JAXTON: OK. Sending you nothing but light.

LOGAN: Thank you.

I have a surprise too. I also got that Native American Heritage Month Awareness Through Art Grant.

JAXTON: Really?

LOGAN: They gave me funding so I could hire a professional actor.

JAXTON: Finally! Thank y—

LOGAN: And I was able to bring the perfect one to town. She elevates the whole project.

JAXTON: Professional actor right here.

LOGAN: Technically, you volunteer for these school plays.

JAXTON: I get paid for that show at the farmers market.

LOGAN: Yeah but you do it on a street corner and are paid in a coffee can.

JAXTON: That is my official performance spot given to me by farmers market security because they understand the importance of teaching about composting.

LOGAN: Jaxton, I value your work, but this woman is from Los Angeles.

JAXTON: Here we go with Los Angeles again. It's not the center of the acting world.

LOGAN: It kind of is.

JAXTON: The *commercial* acting world. Be grateful you didn't make it there. It shows what kind of person you are.

LOGAN: The kind of person who wasn't beautiful enough or sexy enough to compete?

JAXTON: Don't let your head go there, Logan.

LOGAN: Well, wait until you see this actor. She's so beautiful. So L.A.

JAXTON: What is beauty?

LOGAN: A social construct.

JAXTON: That we don't believe in. We value talent and art, not looks. You are a talented actress.

LOGAN: Even better, I'm a director now.
   But I still let my past in L.A. color my present, don't I?

JAXTON: You can't reach new lands until you let go of the shore. Or in this case return to old lands, but as a more enlightened person because of the journey to the other land that was new but is now old and needs to be let go of.

LOGAN: Exactly. I think I can be a mentor to this woman. Help her recover from the false value placed on her sexuality, because I've taken that journey. Show her how much more she can be. Thank you for that self-awareness.

JAXTON: You are one of the most self-aware people I know.

LOGAN: Since knowing you.

JAXTON: I just do my best and hope to Buddha that my karma makes up for the rest of it.

(They kiss.)

LOGAN: It's almost time for rehearsal. We should decouple.

(They separate and perform a decoupling ritual moving from affection to neutral. There is a memorable movement that can be repeated whenever they get too personal.)

JAXTON: Nothing but gender-neutral actor/director respect from here on.
I'll get rid of the cheese.
LOGAN: No, I can handle it.

(Caden enters.)

CADEN: Am I in the right place for rehearsal?
LOGAN: Welcome, Mr. Green. I'm Logan, the director and your fellow collaborator.
CADEN: Please call me Caden. I'm only Mr. Green to my students.
LOGAN: This is Jaxton Smithton. Caden was generously assigned to us by the school district as our history specialist.
JAXTON: You're at Lincoln Elementary, right?
CADEN: I assure you my studies in American History go deeper than the elementary school level.
JAXTON: That's cool, bro. We met at the Let's Learn! Science! tour. I was playing Einstein. You had the student that threw up on my shoes?
CADEN: Actually we met long before that. I've been to Let's Learn! Math! and Let's Learn! Geography! and all of the rest of the Let's Learn! tours.
JAXTON: I don't think we played at Lincoln on the Let's Learn! Math! tour.
CADEN: I took a personal day and saw it at Washington Elementary. I'm a huge fan of your work. *(To Logan)* And I've seen every show you've directed since you got to Jefferson High. *The Iceman Cometh* was made so much more relevant with fifteen year olds.

LOGAN: I appreciate that.

CADEN: It didn't deserve to be shut down.

LOGAN: Three hundred parents disagree.

JAXTON: For now.

LOGAN: I so appreciate your support, Caden.

CADEN: I'm an amateur actor and writer on the side so it is a real thrill to work with professionals like yourselves.

JAXTON: That's awesome, man. Us *professionals* welcome you.

CADEN: I'm especially excited because the email said this is a devised piece. So we're all contributing, right?

LOGAN: Yes. But as the director I have the final say in the construction.

CADEN: This is a dream come true for me.

LOGAN: I'm going to rely on you quite a bit. History is not my strength.

We're waiting on one more actor. Have some refreshments while I text her.

JAXTON: Some cheese, Caden?

(Logan grabs her phone to text as Alicia runs in. The men check her out.)

ALICIA: So sorry I'm late. My Uber app disappeared and the place where I'm staying has terrible reception and I couldn't find the internet password so I had to take a bus. Have you ever taken a bus? It's impossible. I mean literally, it is not possible.

CADEN: I think the word you want is "figuratively" not "literally."

ALICIA: What?

CADEN: Because you're here. So it wasn't "literally" impossible. It's a common mistake.

ALICIA: Are you the director?

LOGAN: No, I am.

(Alicia pointedly turns away from Caden.)

We met at your Skype audition.

ALICIA: I thought you were the casting director.

LOGAN: We don't have casting directors for elementary school shows. I'm the director director.

ALICIA: Oh. I'm Alicia. *(Ah-lee-cee-a)*

LOGAN: Yes, I remember. I hired you. I'm Logan. This is Caden and Jaxton.

ALICIA: Where's my script?

LOGAN: As my email said, we're devising the piece together. That's how I work.

ALICIA: I'm an *actress*.

LOGAN: We work as a team to come up with ideas, try them out, improv some scenes, and then I put the connecting parts in and type it up.

ALICIA: Could I come back when there's a script? I just got to town and have a hundred things to do. And there's the bus. Figuratively.

CADEN: The bus itself is literal.

LOGAN: The devising process is meant to empower the actors.

ALICIA: Do I get paid extra for empowerment?

LOGAN: No. But I want you to know that your voice is the most important one in this play. More important than mine. We could not do this without you.

ALICIA: Really?

JAXTON: Really?

LOGAN: Absolutely. And, personally, I'm here for you.

ALICIA: OK, I'll try it.

CADEN: Is this how you created all of your shows?

JAXTON: It's been a dream of ours to get to do a fully devised educational play. It's the wave of the future in theater. I mean actors in Sweden haven't touched a script in years. They're so far ahead of us.

ALICIA: Ikea is in Sweden, right?

CADEN: Yes.

ALICIA: I love Ikea!

CADEN: Me too. Everything in my apartment is Ikea. Except my mattress and appliances. And the toilet. But everything else.

JAXTON: We all got sucked in, but now we realize what a huge environmental disaster it is to ship boxed packages all over the world when we can buy local.

CADEN: Oh. Yeah.

LOGAN: Anyway, let's get started.

CADEN: I combed through all of my research from grad school and came up with some ideas. Did my homework. *(Chuckles)*

LOGAN: Let's start with your research then. Good drama is at its core, truth.

CADEN: I suggest we begin four thousand years ago when the ancient northern Europeans joined the agricultural revolution and reaped their first organized harvest as farmers. In order to give thanks to the gods for this new way of life they feasted with ceremonies. Thousands of years later those ceremonies become known as the modern Harvest Home Festival.

ALICIA: I thought we're doing a Thanksgiving play.

JAXTON: Another option is to focus on the fact that this is a November play.

ALICIA: Right. For Thanksgiving.

JAXTON: For Native American Heritage Month.

ALICIA: We're performing at something called the All School Turkey Trot. Not the Buffalo Teepee Trot.

JAXTON: It's not my place to tell you how to express yourself, but sound waves travel you know.

LOGAN: As our Native American compass, Alicia is allowed to say what she wants about it.

(Alicia flips her hair.)

JAXTON: Native American?

LOGAN: I told you we got that Heritage Month grant. To hire the professional actor.

JAXTON: You didn't say it was for a Native American actor.

LOGAN: I thought it was implied.

JAXTON *(To Alicia)*: I'm so sorry. It is truly an honor to work with you. I have always been drawn to your ways.

ALICIA: You're a fan of my work?

JAXTON: More than a fan. I'm a devoted follower.

ALICIA: That's sweet. I just opened a new Instagram account. You should follow that one too.

JAXTON: I will.

LOGAN: Now is a good time to mention that in the interest of full disclosure, there are many factors, grant and school board requirements that we need to fulfill with this piece, including Thanksgiving. I am a vegan so that subject is especially sensitive for me. However I want to lift up the acknowledgment that although my sensitivity about the slaughter of millions of animals, including forty-five million turkeys, is valid, I am conscious of not allowing my personal issues to take up more space in the room than the justified anger of the Native people around this idea of Thanksgiving in our post-colonial society. I want to make that crystal clear. Especially for you, Alicia.

ALICIA: Um . . . OK.

LOGAN: If there is anything you want to say on the subject, please know we are holding that space for you.

ALICIA: I'm good right here.

LOGAN: OK. This bit of research is great, Caden, and helps fulfill my Excellence in Education Grant. But I wonder if the best place to start a forty-five-minute Thanksgiving play for elementary grades is four thousand years ago?

ALICIA: Yeah, America didn't even exist.

JAXTON: Better times. That makes me wonder if using the word of the conqueror, "American," could be a trigger for people? What word do you prefer for naming this physical space? I've heard "Turtle Island" used a lot. Do you prefer that?

ALICIA: I like turtles.

LOGAN: Thanks for lifting up that awareness, Jaxton. Coded language is an issue we need to be conscious of, especially when dealing with the next generation.

ALICIA: I don't get codes.

JAXTON: Because that's Navajo.

CADEN: My next idea is pretty cool. Harvest Home Festival is a direct line that can easily be drawn to our modern Thanksgiving celebration. See, I propose that we open on a huge bonfire with ancient Northern European ancestors dancing and feasting on one side and—this is the exciting part—ancient Native American people doing the exact same thing on the other side!

ALICIA: I don't get it.

CADEN: Of course they weren't called "Native American" then. Coded language, thank you, Alicia. We show that both these cultures were already celebrating harvests on both sides of the Atlantic. Two peoples on a parallel track for centuries before they collided as settlers and Wampanoags. History is so dynamic. I mean it's really perfect for theater.

LOGAN: Yes. It is. I'm feeling your passion and I love that. But here's the reality, it's just the three of you.

CADEN: OK.

LOGAN: And it's a school show. Like all the other ones you've seen. So . . . fire won't fly.

CADEN: Then I'm not clear how you plan to depict anything, even up to the "traditionally" recognized Thanksgiving, since all of their lighting, cooking, and warmth was fire.

LOGAN: We're going to have to imagine that part.

CADEN: But your email said we are going to do something revolutionary in educational theater.

JAXTON: We're aiming for a revolution of ideas.

CADEN: So, we open on the two civilizations having feasts on opposite sides of . . . the imaginary fire?

LOGAN: Let's put that in the simmering pot for now.

CADEN: But to make it simmer—

LOGAN: Let's move forward in history. What can we do to break down the myths and stereotypes of Thanksgiving in forty-five minutes with three people? Create a revolution in their minds?

ALICIA: Forty-five minutes seems kinda long.

LOGAN: Well, it's a play. So, actually it's quite short.

ALICIA: But an average show at Disneyland is twenty minutes. That's what they think kids can handle.

LOGAN: Um, we can consider that point of view, but I don't think Disney—

ALICIA: If anyone knows kids, it's Disneyland. It's like science to them. I know, I was the third understudy for Jasmine.

JAXTON: Isn't she Middle Eastern?

ALICIA: My look is super flexible.

JAXTON: Oh yeah, I totally get that.

LOGAN: I hear you, Alicia, but the standard commission from this school district is for a forty-five-minute show, so we should probably trust that they know a little something about children. Even if they do feed them slaughtered flesh and genetically enhanced garbage every day.

ALICIA: I guess.

LOGAN: Caden, what can you tell us about the first recognized Thanksgiving in America?

CADEN: I imagined the third scene three thousand and five hundred years after the first.

LOGAN: What year?

CADEN: 1565.

LOGAN: That sounds close.

CADEN: In Saint Augustine, Florida.

ALICIA: The Pilgrims landed in Florida? I did not know that. So that's why Disneyworld is there? Because it was the original crossroads of the world?

CADEN: Saint Augustine was a settlement of hundreds of Spanish people led by Pedro Menéndez.

ALICIA: I might be a little bit Spanish! Para Español, oprima numero dos.

CADEN: This Thanksgiving was a mass to celebrate a safe journey. Pedro ordered that the Native people be fed as an act of good will. Fun fact. Because they just came from Puerto Rico, it is likely that there were tropical fruits at the first feast instead of yams and squash.

JAXTON: So, you want us to celebrate Native American Heritage Month with a play about Spanish people holding a Catholic mass and eating pineapples?

CADEN: That's just one scene.

LOGAN: The missionaries, Catholicism specifically, are difficult subjects for Indigenous people.

CADEN: But it's true.

JAXTON: Seriously?

LOGAN: Can we jump ahead to New England?

CADEN: But the scene of the next recognized Thanksgiving happens thirty years later in Texas.

ALICIA: OMG. There were Pilgrims in Texas too?

CADEN: An expedition of five hundred Spanish people crossed the desert from Mexico to Texas. Men, women, children, and animals died along the way. Finally, they made it to the Rio Grande. However, many of the people were so overcome with excitement to find water that they rushed into the river and drowned.

JAXTON: Gotta admit, did not see that coming.

CADEN: Those that remained, gave thanks.

LOGAN: How is this appropriate for children?

CADEN: The local Indigenous people joined them and caught fish for the feasting.

LOGAN: From the Rio Grande?

CADEN: I assume so.

ALICIA: Ew.

CADEN: People in El Paso still celebrate that feast as the first Thanksgiving. Only it's in April.

LOGAN: Caden, are we getting close to the normal Thanksgiving? The relatively happy one? In November.

CADEN: That's my next series of proposed scenes. But I warn you, there is drama galore. At least four different dates are vying for the privilege of being "first." And the reasons behind the feast are incredibly varied. From the gruesome—

LOGAN: Worse than eating fish that ate your drowned friends?

CADEN: Much worse. To speculation that the entire Thanksgiving story is a fiction concocted to celebrate the victory of capitalism over communism.

JAXTON: So far all of these stories are coming from the non-Indigenous point of view. I think we need to hold space for the Native perspective.

ALICIA: That's my role.

LOGAN: Alicia, what were you told about the first Thanksgiving in your family?

ALICIA: Well, not much really. I mean we aren't religious or anything.

JAXTON: Of course not.

ALICIA: We just ate food and watched games. We didn't talk about it much.

LOGAN: Maybe we could do something with that? Use play as a universal way to connect with the kids instead of those tired children's songs we make them sing every year.

JAXTON: What kinds of games?

ALICIA: Just the ones that everyone watches.

LOGAN: Right. Is there any chance we could learn about these games with you, as a cast?

ALICIA: I guess. I think the Chiefs are playing Monday, right?

JAXTON: There's a whole game just for chiefs? That's amazing. How many are there?

ALICIA: The same number as any team I guess. I don't really know football that well. It was just on in the background.

JAXTON: Wait, football?

ALICIA: Sure. What do you watch?

(They laugh uneasily.)

LOGAN: NFL football. Well, not anymore, but . . .

JAXTON: This is a perfect example of the exotification of your people. We assumed that you were watching Native American lacrosse or something, instead of allowing you to just be contemporary people. Of course your family watched football. Whose didn't?

CADEN: Mine didn't.

LOGAN: I can't believe we did that. Sorry, Alicia.

ALICIA: We did do one different thing on Thanksgiving. It came from my mom's people.

LOGAN: Do you mind sharing it with us?

JAXTON: Maybe we could get permission to incorporate it into the play? Respectfully.

ALICIA: First we'd buy an extra frozen turkey, a small one, and leave it in the freezer. Then before dinner all the kids would go out to the driveway and set up these wood blocks like bowling pins. Then we'd take turns rolling the frozen turkey at the pins and see who could knock down the most.

JAXTON: Like bowling?

LOGAN: With a frozen turkey?

ALICIA: Yeah that's what they called it, Frozen Turkey Bowling. It was hilarious. Your hands would be freezing so you'd just chuck the thing and it would go all over the driveway. They call them Butterballs, but really, they're not shaped like balls.

LOGAN: This is your family tradition?

ALICIA: My mom grew up in Iowa, so it probably worked better there because it was cold. In L.A. it would start melting and get all mushy and runny.

(Logan looks like she is going to puke.)

LOGAN: Oh my God.

JAXTON: Deep breaths.

LOGAN: We really want to honor your voice and your people's. I just realized that I never asked who your people are.

ALICIA: Um . . . you mean my family?

LOGAN: What are they called?

ALICIA: Well my dad's side is the Longs and my mom's is Hogan. But I use my middle name as my last name for acting. It makes it so I can play all kinds of people.

JAXTON: Can I ask something in all respect?

ALICIA: I guess.

JAXTON: Isn't that problematic? I mean, we're all becoming aware of redface. Doesn't it worry you to be playing other races?

ALICIA: My agent had me take headshots as six different ethnic people, which got me many roles such as Jasmine.

JAXTON: How do you even take headshots as ethnicities? What does that look like?

ALICIA: Different hair, accessories. My Native American shot has me in braids and a turquoise necklace.

JAXTON: Native Americans need to take "Native American" headshots? That seems wrong.

ALICIA: Every actress in L.A. has different types of shots. My agent told me to.

LOGAN: I wouldn't do everything your agent says.

ALICIA: He's my former agent now so I don't do anything he says. Besides Native Americans like invented turquoise so I don't see why wearing it in a shot would piss them off. It's paying them respect.

LOGAN: Them who?

ALICIA: The Native Americans.

LOGAN: But you're them.

ALICIA: Who?

LOGAN: Native American.

ALICIA: I *play* Native American.

JAXTON: You're not Native American?

ALICIA: I'm English and French and a little Spanish we think.

LOGAN: But I hired you to be the Native American.

ALICIA: Yeah.

LOGAN: But you aren't?

ALICIA: No.

LOGAN: But you were my cultural compass.

ALICIA: You hired me to be an actress. Don't worry, I'm gonna act my ass off.

LOGAN: But that's why your voice was so important.

ALICIA: My voice is the most important. You said so.

LOGAN: Because I thought you were Native American.

ALICIA: So non–Native American voices aren't important?

JAXTON: Didn't you wonder why we were asking your advice on all of this stuff?

ALICIA: Because it's *devised*.

LOGAN: But we need a Native American person to do this play. I got a grant.

ALICIA: Look, you hired me off my Native American headshot, so that's on you. You can't fire me because of this. It's a law.

LOGAN: So we're four white people making a culturally sensitive First Thanksgiving play for Native American Heritage Month? Oh my Goddess.

(Jaxton reaches out to comfort her, she pulls away.)

ALICIA: Whatever, it's theater. We don't need actual Native Americans to tell a Native American story. I mean, none of us are actual Pilgrims are we?

CADEN: Interestingly, they didn't call themselves Pilgrims at all. That's a name given to them—

ALICIA: The point is, we're actors. We act. That's the job. Is Lumière a real candlestick?

JAXTON: Actually he kind of was.

ALICIA: Was Grandmother Willow a real willow?

CADEN: She's animated so—

ALICIA: In the Disneyland show?

CADEN: No?

ALICIA: Exactly. And that whole Pocahontas cast was Filipino. We shared a green room.

JAXTON: Do you have any non-Disney references in your life?

LOGAN: I could lose my job over this.

CADEN: I don't think that Alicia playing Native will be a problem with the school district. There are schools that are nearly all black, all Hispanic. If they tried to find ethnic-specific roles for everyone to play, they wouldn't be able to produce anything.

LOGAN: I know about color-blind casting, Caden, I'm the drama teacher. There are grants at stake! A lot of them. And the petition! If I'm not a director or an educator I'm . . . nothing. I'm—

JAXTON: Lo, stay in *this* moment.

LOGAN: But this moment sucks. Take five!

(Everyone disperses.)

SCENE THREE

ACTOR: A selection from songsforteachers.org.

(Can be sung or recited. Perhaps as turkeys:)

ALL:

> Four little turkeys standing in a row.
> First little turkey said, "I don't want to grow."
> Second little turkey said, "What do you know?"
> Third little turkey said, "Thanksgiving is near."
> Fourth little turkey said, "Yes, that's what I hear."
> Then the four little turkeys that were standing in a row,
> All said together . . .
> "Come on, let's go!"
>
> Two little Indians foolin' with a gun,
> One shot t'other and then there was one;

One little Indian left all alone;
He went out and hanged himself and then there were none.

Four fat turkeys sitting on the gate.
The first one said, "Oh my, it's getting late!"
The second one said, "Thanksgiving is our fate."
The third one said, "Here comes the farmer with his gun!"
All said together . . .
"Run, run, run!"

(They scatter. Bam! Bam! Bam! As each gunshot is heard another turkey "dies." One is left alone. She dodges right, left, ducks, and finally . . . Bam! She's down.)

ACTOR: Teacher's comment: For fun, try having students sing "Injun" instead of "Indian." My students loved it.

SCENE FOUR

Alicia and Caden have snacks.

CADEN: So you just moved here?

ALICIA: Yeah.

CADEN: What part of town are you in?

ALICIA: I don't know.

CADEN: I grew up here. If you want to know anything about anything, I can probably tell you.

ALICIA: Anything?

CADEN: Anything about this town.

ALICIA: Oh.

CADEN: But if there's anything else you want to know about, I could look it up for you. I'm really good at research.

ALICIA: That's sweet.

CADEN: Do you want my number or whatever?

ALICIA: I don't know if I'll be here long.

CADEN: Don't like to count your chickens before they hatch?

ALICIA: I thought we're doing turkeys.

(She eats her snacks then looks at the ceiling. Caden goes over his notes.

Jaxton joins Logan.)

LOGAN: I've already screwed this up.

JAXTON: We can fix it. I looked over your Native American Heritage Month grant, and it doesn't explicitly say you have to use it for a Native American person.

LOGAN: Really?

JAXTON: As long as we do something that honors Native Americans for November, you're good to keep the money.

LOGAN: That doesn't seem right. Besides I really wanted to have a Native American voice in this play.

JAXTON: Didn't you check her enrollment card or something?

LOGAN: It's illegal to ask about ethnic, gender, or religious identification in the hiring process. Which I totally support.

JAXTON: But it was pretty obvious that she's not Native.

LOGAN: You thought she was.

JAXTON: I could tell something was off. She's not centered enough. If it's so important to you, we can add a Native actor. A real one.

LOGAN: None applied.

JAXTON: I find it hard to believe there aren't any Native American actors around here.

LOGAN: Have you ever seen one? I don't have the time or resources to go door to door to find one. Alicia cost a lot of money.

It's harder to be a mentor to her than I thought it would be.

JAXTON: She does have a ton of conventional beauty and sex appeal.

LOGAN: Jaxton!

JAXTON: I'm not saying I'm into that, but she has a lot to overcome. It will take time.

LOGAN: Despite all that, do you think we could still use her as Native American and call it color-blind casting?

JAXTON: I think we could get away with using her a few years ago, but now we're post the post-racial society. We can't be blind to differences.

LOGAN: Right. Before we were blind to race but now we totally see it. It's our duty as allies.

JAXTON: Yes. And as allies we need to say something for those who can't be here to speak for themselves.

LOGAN: Or, is it as allies we need to be sure they are here to speak for themselves?

JAXTON: That's what I'm saying.

LOGAN: So if they aren't here, does anyone speak for them?

JAXTON: I don't think we're supposed to speak for anyone but ourselves.

LOGAN: Right. So, we just speak for white people?

JAXTON: I think so. We see color but we don't speak for it.

LOGAN: Which means Alicia can't play Native American, for sure?

JAXTON: Definitely not.

LOGAN: But can we really say that? Then we're speaking for Native American people who aren't here.

JAXTON: Maybe we should tell a Native American person and see if they say it.

LOGAN: Yes of course. *(Thinks)* But I don't know any Native Americans.

JAXTON: A guy in my yoga class built a sweat lodge on his deck, so he probably knows a local Native American person. He made it totally traditional.

LOGAN: That means he used dead animal skin to cover it, didn't he?

JAXTON: Yes, but it's all up-cycled leather from jackets he gets on Etsy.

LOGAN: That helps.

But your friend's not Native American?

JAXTON: No, he learned how to build it at Burning Man. But I'm sure he's had a Native American person to the lodge. Wait, he's at a yoga retreat in Machu Picchu. No phones allowed.

LOGAN: Well then, I guess in the absence of any Native American people, we should make a decision, for the good of the school system, so they don't get in trouble.

JAXTON: Right, then we're technically still speaking on behalf of white people because we're speaking for the school administration.

LOGAN: Yes. That sounds right. We're white people speaking for white people.

JAXTON: OK.

LOGAN: We can do that.

JAXTON: Absolutely.

LOGAN *(To the group)*: We're back people. After some thinking, I have decided that we cannot use non–Native American people to play Native American characters.

CADEN: So there won't be any Native Americans in a Thanksgiving play for Native American Month?

JAXTON: It's the right thing to do.

ALICIA: What part will I play?

LOGAN: A Pilgrim.

ALICIA: But I'm maybe part Spanish so I should have the biggest parts in the Florida and Texas stories.

LOGAN: We aren't going to do those stories.

ALICIA: Why not?

CADEN: Yes, why not?

LOGAN: Because there aren't any white people in them and we've got a cast of white people.

ALICIA: In this country if you're part anything else, you're not white. It's a drop thing. *(To Caden)* If I'm Spanish I'm not white, right?

CADEN: I think that depends on the region of origin. I'm not an expert on—

(Alicia gives him a look.)

I'll do the research and get back to you.

LOGAN: The ethical thing to do is to play what we know we are.

ALICIA: I was promised a large part.

LOGAN: My Gender Equity in History Grant requires a lead female historical figure, so that will be you.

ALICIA: Good.

LOGAN: This is a challenge, but we are the future of theater and education. Are we all in agreement?

JAXTON: Support.

ALICIA: *Main* Pilgrim.

LOGAN: Yes. Caden?

CADEN: I'll defend you to the school board if I have to.

LOGAN: OK then, no Native Americans in our Thanksgiving play. Let's start with an improv. We'll use the traditional story we all know. Just see where it goes.

CADEN: That story isn't necessarily historically accurate.

LOGAN: We need to get our creative juices flowing and figure out what our options are to celebrate Native Americans without them. Let's act.

(Jaxton, Alicia and Caden turn in circles a bit, not sure where to face.)

ALICIA: Which way is downstage?

LOGAN: It doesn't matter in an improv. You just react.

(They wander a bit, not able to define a space.)

Let's put the audience here.

(They all face Logan downstage and fall into line.)

You're at a Pilgrim's house preparing the meal for the first Thanksgiving.

(They move chairs around.)

ALICIA: I feel like it's my house.

LOGAN: Fine. Let's leave the rest of the discoveries for the improv.

(They mime preparing foods. Perhaps too graphically.)

JAXTON: Wait. Didn't we get this food from Native American people?

ALICIA: Yeah, isn't that the whole point of Thanksgiving? To thank the Native people for saving us from . . . something . . . with food?

CADEN: Starvation.

ALICIA: We should totally thank them for that.

JAXTON: Why are we fixing this food if it was a gift?

LOGAN: The Pilgrims must have done some of the actual preparation.

JAXTON: But without any Native American people to guide them?

CADEN: Actually—

LOGAN: OK, you're sitting down to eat the dinner that is already prepared.

(Alicia sits across from Jaxton and Caden. They mime eating with various levels of mime proficiency.)

ALICIA: Would you like more stuffing?

CADEN: Stuffing is a modern dish. A more likely side considering the efficiency of the early settlers would be a type of sweetbreads or pâté.

LOGAN: Caden, we call improv a world of yes. We don't judge or try to make sense of choices, we simply say "yes" and see where it leads us.

CADEN: So sorry. *(To Alicia)* Yes, I would love some, what did you call it? Stuffing?

ALICIA: I was mistaken. It's corn. Native American corn.

CADEN: Thank you.

JAXTON: This meal is wonderful.

ALICIA: Without our Native American neighbors . . . in the next room, we would be dead. From starvation.

CADEN *(Pleased)*: Yes. We owe them thanks.

ALICIA: I thanked them.

JAXTON: Good.

(They mime-eat in silence. For a while.)

ALICIA: We should say a prayer of Thanksgiving.

LOGAN: Public schools.

ALICIA: What?

LOGAN: We can't pray in public schools.

ALICIA *(To Caden)*: Pilgrims are religious. Right?

CADEN: Yes!

ALICIA: Brother Jaxton, would you say a prayer of thanks?

JAXTON: O . . . K. Um . . . Dear . . . Father. Shouldn't we wait to say the prayer until our Native . . . um . . . brothers— What should we call them?

LOGAN: Indigenous people?

CADEN: The truth is in the writings from this time, they were referred to as "savages." But we can't say that in a school show. We could call them "the Natives." As in they are native to this land.

JAXTON: OK. But my point was going to be, we should have our Native brothers in the room to say the Thanksgiving prayer.

ALICIA: Yes. Let's wait for them. More . . . vegetable?

CADEN: Thank you.

(More mime. Silence.)

LOGAN: And scene. We can't pray, and we can't do a hero story without the hero.

JAXTON: It's weird.

CADEN: Somehow we need Indians.

(They think.)

ALICIA: A dream sequence.

JAXTON: How does that help?

ALICIA: My character can dream that she is a Native person. And I'll play me because it's my dream.

CADEN: I think that's still redface.

ALICIA: I'm not Native. I'm a Pilgrim dreaming Native. It's totally different.

CADEN: Well . . .

JAXTON: Technically she would still be in redface, but we're not hiding that she's in redface.

LOGAN: It's meta, so maybe it's OK.

JAXTON: I think so.

ALICIA: Why are you the ones who get to decide everything?

LOGAN: As enlightened white allies, Jaxton and I have put a lot of thought into these issues.

JAXTON: Like every day of our lives. We can't escape our whiteness.

ALICIA: But I play white. I can decide things too.

JAXTON: Yeah, but I'm a straight. White. Male. It's an endless minefield.

CADEN: I'm straight too. Funnily, I am Italian which used to be considered ethnic but is now white.

JAXTON: Whoa, this whole thing must be bringing up a lot of sensitivity issues for you. For being one of Christopher Columbus's bros.

CADEN: I'm not related to Columbus.

JAXTON: But you have the awareness that your people started the slavery and genocide of millions.

CADEN: That's not all Columbus did.

JAXTON: You're balancing karma. We uplift the celebration of Native American Heritage Month, and Columbus Day inches a little closer to oblivion.

CADEN: Well, Columbus Day is actually a celebration of the contributions of Italians to—

JAXTON: Then why not Mussolini Day? Or—

LOGAN: Focus people. The new idea on the table is that Alicia will dream that she is Native American, thus allowing a Native point of view in the piece. Do we have consensus?

JAXTON: I guess.

CADEN: Yes.

ALICIA: You know what would be great? If it was like me talking to myself. Like Native me talking to Pilgrim me. Helping me see the beauty and bounty of this land.

(Jaxton pulls out his phone and looks at it through the following:)

LOGAN: So you are proposing that this whole section is just you?

ALICIA: I can tell the other characters about my dream in the morning.

LOGAN: Then it's just monologues.

ALICIA: Some amazing plays are mostly monologues. Like *The Vagina Monologues.*

CADEN: As an elementary school teacher I can say with authority that monologues put children to sleep. Sorry.

JAXTON: What we need is conflict. I was just googling, and things weren't so chill between the Pilgrims and the Indians. I mean, obviously, the Pilgrims were land stealers like Columbus. But they were totally in the middle of some very specific battles.

ALICIA: So you guys can battle Native me in my dream.

JAXTON: Or we can all be white people, Pilgrims, preparing for a battle. War is intense. Kids dig that.

CADEN: I brought a dramatic, post-battle scene that only involves white people, technically.

JAXTON: Sweet.

LOGAN: We're celebrating violence?

JAXTON: Maybe my character is conflicted about fighting the Indians. *(To Alicia)* Good wife, I'm so conflicted about the impending war.

(She slides up next to him, very cozy.)

ALICIA: Let me soothe you, dear husband.

LOGAN: Maybe she's your sister! Or your platonic friend?

ALICIA: Oh, you're a couple. I did not get that.

LOGAN: Jaxton and I share a mutually respectful relationship.

ALICIA: So you aren't a couple?

LOGAN: New plan. We are going to divide and conquer. Sorry. Alicia and I will work on her dream idea. Jaxton and Caden work on the battle idea.

JAXTON: Wait. Isn't it inappropriate for us to split along gender lines?

CADEN: I'll work with Alicia.

LOGAN: But is it more inappropriate for us to intentionally not split along gender lines?

JAXTON: I don't know.

LOGAN: The impetus was creative interest, so I think it's OK.

JAXTON: But two men doing the war stuff? Isn't that playing into gender assumptions that we want to disrupt?

LOGAN: But it's period so we're being historically accurate.

JAXTON: Right.

LOGAN: Yes.

JAXTON: Sorry.

LOGAN: No, thanks for always being conscious.

CADEN: Are there any props or costumes here?

LOGAN: There's a few.

JAXTON *(To Caden)*: The good stuff is out in the storage closet. Come on.

CADEN: Great.

(The men go.)

LOGAN: Alicia, I want to be sure there are no hard feelings in what just happened with the Native American casting, redface thing. I don't blame you at all, and I hope you understand why we had to make this decision.

ALICIA: You're the director, it's your show.

LOGAN: No, it's our show. Really. I want you to feel as empowered as possible. I've been a female actor in L.A.

ALICIA: You lived in L.A?

LOGAN: For six weeks. My time in L.A. was . . . hard. But since then I've seen how it's not us, as women, but the business that makes us believe in the lies of beauty and sex.

ALICIA: But sex is a real thing.

LOGAN: Yes, but believing that your value is tied to your ability to portray sex and beauty is a lie.

ALICIA: You don't think I'm beautiful?

LOGAN: Well, yes. In the way our society defines beauty and attaches worth to it. I realize now that my own beauty is from the inside. We are all beautiful.

ALICIA: Of course you are.

LOGAN: You see my inner beauty?

ALICIA: No. I mean you're really pretty. You just hide it. But I could help you. It would only take a little makeup to highlight your eyes and add some lift to your hair and you'd be gorgeous.

LOGAN: Not gorgeous.

ALICIA: Sure. Change up the cut of your clothes, add a hair flip, and Jaxton won't be able to keep his hands off you.

LOGAN: I've never understood the hair flip.

ALICIA: It's easy. You just flip.

(She does it. Logan tries to copy her.)

You've got it! It shows your neck. Makes guys want to kiss it.

(Logan recovers herself.)

LOGAN: OK. Enough hair flipping. What I want to tell you is that since L.A., I quit acting because I realized that I could be so much more. I became a director so that I could show off the power of my mind. I'm a teacher so that I can change the future. I have plans, dreams. Jaxton has helped me stay focused on that path and I want to get you on it too.

ALICIA: My boyfriend helped me. But he dropped me from his agency, so I dropped him from my life and moved out.

LOGAN: Good for you.

ALICIA: I mean if he's not getting me work then he's not getting sex. Right?

LOGAN: Um . . . there it is. You certainly should never feel pressured into sex or like it's a commodity.

ALICIA: Not unless I'm getting something good for it.

LOGAN: Well—

ALICIA: You've had sex, right?

LOGAN: Yes. But . . . you know what? As your employer we shouldn't even be talking about this. Now you're going to be a writer. You have so many more options for your future.

ALICIA: Look, I'm not that smart—

LOGAN: Don't say that.

ALICIA: No, really, I'm not. I've been tested. But I know how to make people stare at me and not look away. And when I say something onstage, people listen and they believe me. But this history stuff and writing, I don't know how to do that. So if you want to make me feel empowered or whatever, let me do what I know how to do and don't force me to do something that makes me feel stupid.

LOGAN: But I am here to help you. Teach you.

ALICIA: I don't want to learn.

LOGAN: Seriously?

ALICIA: I'm happy doing my thing.

LOGAN: You have no ambition to be more than an actor?

ALICIA: What's wrong with being an actress?

LOGAN: Nothing. I just—I don't believe I've ever met a person without ambition. Not in any aspect of my life.

ALICIA: I'm ambitious. I want to do more acting.

LOGAN: Wow. You are certainly the most . . . simple person I've ever met.

ALICIA: I'm not smart but I'm definitely not simpleminded.

LOGAN: No. Simplicity is difficult. Multitasking, constantly trying to be something more, everyone does that. But to *be* simplicity, that's unbelievably difficult.

ALICIA: Not really. I just . . . don't do stuff I don't want to do and do the stuff I do.

LOGAN: You're talking directly to me and I can barely wrap my brain around it. I've never, for one moment in my life, been content.

ALICIA: I'm content all the time. Except when my agent dropped me, but then I dumped him and felt fine.

LOGAN: Teach me how to be content.

ALICIA: Right now?

LOGAN: Please. You have no idea how stressed I am. But if I can get my reputation back with the parents and they withdraw that petition, next year I could— See, I'm doing it already. I'm already worried about next year's production and we just started this one. Help me be content with this moment I'm in. We're in, together.

ALICIA: Well, basically you don't do anything.

LOGAN: That's it?

ALICIA: Like normally in rehearsal if they are working on someone else's scene, I just sit here. Or play Angry Birds on my phone, but I forgot my charger so I don't want to wear down the battery.

LOGAN: So you meditate? Or think about . . . what?

ALICIA: Nothing. Sometimes I'll look out the window. Or I'll study the ceiling. People leave you alone when you study the ceiling.

LOGAN: OK.

ALICIA: So now we just do it.

LOGAN: Now?

ALICIA: Uh-huh.

(Alicia sits back and stares at the ceiling. Logan studies her a bit then tries to do the same.)

LOGAN: Do you count tiles or . . .

ALICIA: Nope, just stare at it.

LOGAN: Right.

(Logan struggles to keep staring.)

I can't turn my brain off.

ALICIA: Maybe you're too smart to be content.

LOGAN: I am smart. I've been tested too.

ALICIA: I can tell.

LOGAN: So I can't be content?

ALICIA: I've never seen a smart person that is.

LOGAN: You're a lucky woman, Alicia.

ALICIA: I think so.

LOGAN: You're also wise. You're sure you're not Native American?

ALICIA: Yep. Do you want me to work on my dream monologues?

LOGAN: No, you don't have to write anything.

ALICIA: Cool.

LOGAN: I need a break. Keep doing . . . nothing.

ALICIA: Got it.

(Alicia resumes staring at the ceiling as Logan goes. The men return.)

JAXTON: Logan, are there any swords in here?

LOGAN: No.

CADEN: Period rifles?

LOGAN: Nope.

CADEN: We'll have to make do.

(Logan goes as the men shuffle through Caden's papers.)

SCENE FIVE

Two actors sing as a period white person (Pilgrim, western, etc.) and a Native. Perhaps add additional songs in the style of "This Land Is Your Land," etc.

ACTOR 1: Youtube.com/eastsidemiddleschoolfortheperforming
arts/thanksgivingassembly.

NATIVE *(Tune: "Home on the Range")*:
 Oh give me a home where the buffalo roam,
 Where the deer and the antelope play,
 Where seldom is heard a discouraging word,
 And the skies are not cloudy all day.

WHITE PERSON *(Tune: "Home on the Range")*:
 The red man was pressed
 From this part of the west,
 He's likely no more to return,

To the banks of the Red River
Where seldom if ever
Their flickering campfires burn.

NATIVE *(Tune: "My Country 'Tis of Thee")*:
My country 'tis of thee,
Sweet land of liberty,
Of thee I sing.
Land where my fathers died!

WHITE PERSON *(Tune: "My Country 'Tis of Thee")*:
Land of the Pilgrim's pride!
From every mountainside,

NATIVE AND WHITE PERSON:
Let freedom ring!

ACTOR 1: Public comment: Nine months ago. Are those really the lyrics? The "red man"? That's horrible.
ACTOR 2: Look it up, it's historical. Quit being so sensitive.

SCENE SIX

CADEN: But without the battle scene first—

JAXTON: Trust me, I think the real impact is in the scene after the battle. Back at the fort.

CADEN: Colony.

JAXTON: The Pilgrim Palace.

CADEN: Actually, it was quite spartan.

JAXTON: Seriously, man, you gotta loosen up on the facts.

CADEN: But facts are . . . facts. They don't loosen or tighten. They just are.

JAXTON: For now we gotta zero in on a compelling story, then we'll put all the facts in that you think we need, OK?

CADEN: Fine.

JAXTON: You've got a lot of scenes here.

CADEN: Thanks. Playwriting is a secret dream of mine.

JAXTON: You told us that in like the first two minutes.

CADEN: You're the only ones that know. And all of my students.

JAXTON: Gotta give voice to your dreams. Speak your truth and it will become truth.

CADEN: Well, I don't know that it actually works like—

JAXTON: Facts kill dreams.

CADEN: Well . . .

JAXTON: Do you know what I said I wanted to be when I grow up? An actor slash yoga dude.

CADEN: Like teach yoga?

JAXTON: Just be yoga. People told me that was crazy. It's not a "real" profession. But I said it anyway and here I am. I act and I do yoga. I spoke my truth. It became truth.

CADEN: That's seriously all you do?

JAXTON: Those are my passions.

CADEN: You get paid for your passions?

JAXTON: I have a day job, but that's not what's important in the story of me. Look, this homecoming scene of yours is the key

CADEN: I don't think Logan will like it.

JAXTON: It's a devised piece. She doesn't have to like everything.

(Logan returns. Perhaps she has cleaned up a bit, added some lipstick. Something Alicia.)

Lo, we've got a scene that has me so stoked.

LOGAN: Wow. That was fast. Great.

JAXTON: Caden's got like a whole play written. It just needs a little trimming and we could do it. Devising process done.

LOGAN: But what about our input?

CADEN: I can work in whatever Alicia's got.

ALICIA: Logan said I don't have to write anything. I'm being simplicity.

CADEN: Ummm . . .

LOGAN: I'm supporting Alicia in staying with her strengths. She knows what she does well and I want to honor that.

It's so . . . brave and Zen really. Jaxton, she has absolutely no desire to be more. She's like you but way further down the path because she doesn't have intellect in her way.

JAXTON: Wait, like me?

LOGAN: Free. You yoga and sometimes act and just live. Alicia just acts. Nothing else.

ALICIA: I do do stuff. Sometimes.

LOGAN: But you don't *need* to do stuff. I'm telling you, Jaxton. It's genius. Only she's not. That's not being offensive, she's been tested.

ALICIA: It's true.

LOGAN: I had it all wrong. She is here to mentor us.

JAXTON: Well, our scene is incredibly . . . simplicity. It strikes at the core of the Native American gestalt with one visual. It's quite brilliant.

CADEN: Thank you, Jaxton.

JAXTON: There's lots of clunky educational dialogue but we'll fix that.

CADEN: Oh.

(Jaxton grabs his props, a bag with something large in it, and various costume pieces. He nods to Caden.)

The year is 1631. Upon landing in Cape Cod the Separatists, now known as Pilgrims, immediately robbed the graves and nearly all of the food stores of the local Natives. However, with the help of Samoset, the English-speaking Native who had escaped slavery, a tenuous treaty was drawn. But, six years and many ships later, when the Separatists discovered a white man dead on a boat in Plymouth they assumed the Native people had killed him. Major John Mason—

(Jaxton steps forward.)

gathered his men and surrounded an unsuspecting Pequot village. They killed four hundred Native men, women, and children. Major Mason and his men came home to give thanks and celebrate their victory.

JAXTON: Do not fear good, God-fearing folk. We have in short order laid waste to the savage villains. Prepare a feast most glorious and give thanks to God, for he hath delivered our resounding victory. I bring forth the trophies of our labors.

(Out of his bag he pulls two crafted heads that have long, dark hair. They are oozing a red blood-like liquid. He drops them on the ground. Blood sprays.)

LOGAN: Wait. Are those heads?

CADEN: Native American heads.

JAXTON: We shall give sport with the heads of our enemies on this day of thanks.

CADEN: Yes we shall!

(Jaxton kicks a head to Caden.)

LOGAN: Oh my God!

ALICIA: I wanna play!

(They ad-lib as they toss and kick the heads between them. Something is knocked over, Logan is horrified.)

LOGAN: Don't touch that, Alicia!

ALICIA: Frozen Turkey Bowling!

(Alicia jumps up and rolls a head into something. Heads fly around the stage, leaving blood everywhere.)

LOGAN: STOP!!

(They stop.)

Have you lost your minds? How is killing off hundreds of Indigenous people, then kicking their heads, a proper celebration of Native American Heritage Month?

CADEN: It's true, and gets a Native American presence into our play.

JAXTON: It's like those programs in high school where they make you visit a prison to stay out of prisons and see a crashed car to stay out of drunk driver cars and visit a morgue to . . . stay out of morgues.

LOGAN: This is appalling.

JAXTON: But it's real. That's what we need, not a cleansing of history, but an in-your-face reminder that this is what we're capable of or we will keep doing it.

CADEN: Exactly.

LOGAN: If I do a gruesome play where you kick heads for sport, I will lose my job for sure.

JAXTON: But the genocide on Turtle Island is ongoing. If we white people don't admit the horrors of what we did and are still doing, it won't stop.

LOGAN: First off, this is public school, the growing majority of these kids aren't white anyway. Second, petition or not, I will be fired. We aren't doing this. I'm the director. I've decided.

JAXTON: Lo, it's devised theater.

LOGAN: Jaxton, I made it clear from the beginning that in this format I will have final say.

JAXTON: Yeah but—

LOGAN: I said no!

JAXTON: You're being a bitch—bit dictatorial about it.

LOGAN: That is an incredibly offensive gender-biased statement.

JAXTON: I went by the pronoun "they" for a full year. I'm allowed one mistake.

LOGAN: That wasn't a mistake. You've always been jealous of me because I'm a theater professional and you aren't.

JAXTON: You teach high school theater.

LOGAN: You are a street performer.

JAXTON: I'm a local celebrity.

ALICIA: Really?

LOGAN: Actually yes. But I believe that you, as a fellow human, are having difficulty with the inequity of our professional relationship and are lashing out.

(Logan executes a fantastic hair flip. Alicia is proud.)

ALICIA: Good girl.

(Jaxton has a realization.)

JAXTON: Dude. I *am* feeling a tension in my positional relationship to you.

LOGAN: I'm sorry I had to call it out like that.

JAXTON: Whoa. I think this is what "less than" feels like.

LOGAN: I don't think of you as less than me.

JAXTON: You called me a street performer.

LOGAN: Well, you are. But if saying it in that tone offended you I am sorry for the results you felt even though that wasn't my intention.

CADEN: I think it was.

JAXTON: It was. And that is a profound gift. Do you know how hard it is for a straight white male to feel "less than" in this world? I don't know that I've ever truly felt it in my life.

CADEN: I have.

JAXTON: I don't want to lose this feeling. Say it again.

LOGAN: Seriously?

JAXTON: Please, help me, Lo.

LOGAN: Um . . . you're a street performer?

JAXTON: Come on, give it to me.

LOGAN: You're a street performer.

JAXTON: If you care about me, hit me with it.

LOGAN: You're a bad street performer!

JAXTON: Yes!

LOGAN: The school board said I didn't have to hire you but you work for free!

JAXTON: More!

LOGAN: You're a terrible actor.

JAXTON: Hurt me!

LOGAN: And the sex is so—

JAXTON: Back off!

LOGAN: bizarre! Why do you do—

JAXTON: Too far!

LOGAN: Sorry!

JAXTON: I should go meditate on this feeling right now.

LOGAN: Should we talk about . . .

(Jaxton sits to meditate.)

JAXTON: OMMMMMM.

LOGAN: Maybe we should all meditate for a moment.

ALICIA: Umm . . .

LOGAN: Just keep doing nothing.

ALICIA: Got it.

(Logan and Jaxton take meditation positions. Alicia sits back and stares at the ceiling. Caden isn't sure what to do. He tries an asana, not great. Finally, he sits in a chair and puts his head down on a desk.)

SCENE SEVEN

The agitprop version. Don't get too earnest, let the appropriation fly.

ACTOR: Applying social responsibility and ethics to a classroom Thanksgiving. Lesson plan for grades nine through twelve.

ALL:
Where?
Plymouth, Massachusetts.
When?
Thanksgiving 1997.
Who?
The United American Indians of New England.
And the local police.
What?
Since 1970 a National Day of Mourning has been observed with a march at noon.

In 1997 police attempted to disband the march with tear gas and violent arrests.

Twenty-five people were arrested, many injured.

Medical attention was not immediately provided to those under arrest.

The police characterized the protesters as "terrorists" who should be treated accordingly.

Why?

(Silence.)

ACTOR: Final assignment: Have students write letters of apology to the Indians. Then, read them to each other.

SCENE EIGHT

LOGAN: I've got it! Sorry. When you folx are done.

CADEN: I'm good.

ALICIA: Whatever.

JAXTON: Om.

LOGAN: We'll start and Jaxton can join us. I want to try a Pil-grim-style Thanksgiving scene, but we show the actual erasure of Native people. Graphically.

CADEN: I thought the scene with the heads was pretty graphic.

LOGAN: Graphic in a visceral way, not a visual one. We do a first Thanksgiving scene, like normal, with Native people, but we don't play Native people. We allow their absence to speak for them. Where is the missing Indigenous per-spective? It's certainly missing from this room. We hold space for them by literally holding space for them. Give me a few minutes to work out some dialogue.

CADEN: I have a dinner scene I was holding on to. No death or Spaniards. Just the "normal" story we all know.

LOGAN: Let me see it.

(Caden looks through a large stack of pages.)

You actually wrote the whole play didn't you?

CADEN: There's nothing that means more to me in my life than this opportunity.

LOGAN: Thanks for this work. All of it, Caden.

CADEN: Here it is!

(He hands Logan a scene.)

LOGAN: Everyone take a break while I figure this out.

(Logan goes somewhere to work on it.
Jaxton joins Caden and Alicia at the snacks.)

JAXTON: That meditation was deep. I faced a lot about myself and my privilege.

CADEN: I don't know if I could hear my girlfriend say that kind of stuff about me and be OK with it.

JAXTON: I know that her lashing out is not about her and me but actually her double-X's fighting back against centuries of patriarchal oppression. It's not personal. It felt personal for a second, which I totally needed, but intellectually I know to filter anything she says to me through layers of justified feminine rage.

CADEN: So no matter what she says, you don't believe it?

JAXTON: I believe she believes it, but I know to trust myself first. And not everyone is ready for Tantric, right? *(To Alicia)* You play oppressed characters a lot, how do you get in touch with that as a person of privilege?

ALICIA: I imagine I'm that character so I feel what they feel.

JAXTON: But do you use substitution technique from your own life or method or what?

ALICIA: I pretend to be them.

JAXTON: That's it?

ALICIA: Yeah. And I can make myself cry on command.

JAXTON: Like in a scene?

ALICIA: No. Right now.

(Alicia literally cries tears.)

JAXTON: Whoa.

CADEN: That is impressive.

(She stops.)

ALICIA: I list it on my special skills. People ask me to do it in auditions all the time.

JAXTON: I'm getting what Logan was saying about you. You're so . . . simple.

ALICIA: She called me simplicity.

JAXTON: That's it. You should teach workshops. People would dig that.

ALICIA: It seems like either you have simplicity or you don't. Smart people don't get it. I just tried with Logan and she couldn't do it.

JAXTON: So I'm probably too smart?

ALICIA: Maybe. He is for sure.

CADEN: I'm OK with that.

JAXTON: But still, you could charge people money to come listen to you.

ALICIA: That's what I do now. I'm an actress.

JAXTON: You are blowing my mind. Seriously. Mind blown.

ALICIA: No one's ever said that to me before when I had my clothes on.

(Jaxton and Caden register this.)

JAXTON: I can't formulate a response that isn't not misogynistic.

ALICIA: Simplicity.

(Logan rejoins them.)

LOGAN: OK, this is experimental, but that's what I love about theater for kids. You can really do anything and they will follow you. We'll sit around the table of the first Thanksgiving. Our Native friends are at the end.

(They arrange chairs and sit with two empty ones.)

First time through let's read all the lines. I'll read both Samoset and Massasoit.

(She moves back and forth between the chairs as she does Samoset's or Massasoit's lines. Caden tends to mouth the words along with them.)

ALICIA: Good Native king and good interpreter, welcome on this day of the good Lord's Feast of Thanksgiving. What may I offer to make your visit pleasing?

LOGAN: I, Samoset, whilst request more of the fowl your men gathered with their exploding sticks.

ALICIA: Wouldest thou prefer the breast or the leg?

LOGAN: Massasoit, which part of the bird is most pleasing to your countenance? *(Switching chairs as Massasoit)* That which is most succulent pleaseth me.

ALICIA: The breast is ample whilst the leg is moist.

JAXTON: Dear wife, our gratitude is owed these men a thousand times. Please, take the whole between you.

CADEN: Yes, we wouldest have died as did so many of our number.

LOGAN: Scene. Great work everyone.

(Caden is overcome with emotion or heartburn.)

JAXTON: Dude, are you OK?

CADEN: It just hit me. I read my words with real actors. This is the best day of my life!

JAXTON: Most people go their whole lives without living their dreams, but you put yourself out there.

LOGAN: I'm thrilled to facilitate this moment for you, Caden. I'd like to take a second to honor your emotional space.

(They all do.)

And do it again.

CADEN: It would help to hear it with better acting this time. *(To Jaxton and Alicia)* I think some context of why you two are so grateful might help you get the emotional arc—

JAXTON: Not cool.

LOGAN: Caden, it's customary that actors do not give each other notes. Any notes come through the director.

CADEN: Just trying to be helpful. There was something missing last time.

ALICIA: Want me to cry at the end?

CADEN: That would be great.

LOGAN: OK. Let's read it again and see what happens. This time when we get to the Native lines, I won't read them but we look at the space and listen as if the Native characters are there.

ALICIA: But they aren't.

LOGAN: We're pretending.

ALICIA: Oh. I can do that.

Good Native king and good interpreter, welcome on this day of the good Lord's Feast of Thanksgiving. What may I offer to make your visit pleasing?

(They look to a chair in silence. Alicia can't help but go sex-kittenish. It's a reflex. The group's attention is drawn to her like moths to a flame.)

Wouldest thou prefer the breast or the leg?

(Silence again.)

The breast is ample whilst the leg is moist.

(Jaxton bursts into giggles.)

What?

JAXTON: Ample breast, moist legs?

(Alicia laughs.)

CADEN: Only those with juvenile humor would find this pleasant exchange about food humorous.

JAXTON: Our audience is all juveniles.

LOGAN: *Juvenile* humor aside, I think it really worked. Notice how in the moments of silence, we were all totally focused. It was so impactful.

ALICIA: I felt that.

JAXTON: But can we do a whole play like that?

LOGAN: It's applicable to our contemporary situation. Erased presence.

CADEN: Although the acting was great. It wasn't as strong for me as the first time with all of the lines.

LOGAN: This is very early discovery, we're playing.

CADEN: Perhaps we could do it like a ventriloquist. Still keep the visual nothingness, but say their lines. Like this. *(Poorly done ventriloquist voice)* I, Samoset, whilst request more of the fowl your men gathered with their exploding sticks.

JAXTON *(Giggling)*: Exploding sticks. Caden, you horny man. You wrote a sex comedy.

CADEN: I did not!

LOGAN: Please stop talking about sex.

JAXTON: I'm simply naming what's in the room.

LOGAN: It's a children's show.

JAXTON: Caden wrote a sex comedy. And I, as a heteronormative male, recognize and honor the power of Alicia's sacral chakra. *(To Alicia)* Oh yeah, I'll give you something to feast on.

(Alicia catches on and plays the part.)

ALICIA: Partake of my generous bounty, good sir.

JAXTON: Let your rich sauces run down my chin.

ALICIA: Whilst thou have me carve the breast?

JAXTON: Wait, what?

LOGAN: That's enough. Caden, the voice takes away from the idea of erased presence. Know what I mean?

CADEN: I don't think the erased presence works as well as the lines I wrote.

JAXTON: He's right, Lo, the silence is wrong.

LOGAN: Why are you fighting me?

JAXTON: By silencing the Native voices we've made them too strong. Silence is so powerful onstage. Our characters can't compete with that.

LOGAN: But we want the silence to be strong. The nothingness of the Natives is the whole point.

JAXTON: So it's an inequality.

LOGAN: Yes.

JAXTON: Then are we being fair to the Pilgrims?

CADEN: Separatists.

JAXTON: White people.

LOGAN: Aren't we aiming for an equitable world, not a fair world?

JAXTON: You've hit it right in the chakras. By doing this with the silenced voices, we are reinforcing the inequality of humans. Calling out one human as more worthy of attention and power.

LOGAN: But it is Native American Heritage Month. A particular time specified to lift up one people's voice over others.

JAXTON: But do we believe in that or have we played right into a massive blind spot? If you make a month for everyone, will it ever be fair? No. Someone will always be left out. Or get a weird month like Hispanic Heritage Month.

ALICIA: When's Hispanic Heritage Month?

JAXTON: September 15 to October 15.

ALICIA: How is that even a month?

JAXTON: Exactly.

LOGAN: Well it is thirty days.

CADEN: And it coincides with the Independence Days of several Latin American countries.

JAXTON: Come on, how is it equal to give one group a mid-month as their month?

ALICIA: There isn't a white-person month. I checked.

JAXTON: That's what I'm saying. Thank you, Alicia.

LOGAN: Basically every month is white-person month.

JAXTON: But once we are the minority again, will we get an official month? And will that make things right? No. The point is, this whole project is inherently inequitable. By raising up one voice through a month or silence, we are lowering another. That's not what we should be teaching children.

LOGAN: I think we're getting offtrack. My idea—

JAXTON: We have a worksheet for this. To add up privilege so that we can then equalize it.

ALICIA: What is privilege?

LOGAN: The things about you that give you power.

ALICIA: I'm hot. That's power so that's privilege.

LOGAN: Believing your power is only because of your looks is buying into a subjective social construct.

ALICIA: I haven't opened a door or paid for a drink since I was sixteen. Hotness is privilege.

CADEN: I think she's right.

LOGAN: Although I respect your hotness, this talk will get my Go! Girls! Scholastic Leadership funding pulled.

JAXTON: We can talk about your hotness at break, Alicia. Now if we apply the worksheet to Logan's idea . . .

(He works it out on a chalk or white board.)

The white people are visible so that's one point. The Native people have a month and silence so that's two points. The story is written pretty evenly so that's a point to both. See, the silence makes it unequal.

(Alicia studies the math.)

ALICIA: So if one side is silent, to make it equal don't both sides have to be silent?

JAXTON: She might be right. It is the definition of simplicity.

CADEN: No it's not. It's the definition of madness. You can't have a silent play.

JAXTON: Actually, it's been done.

CADEN: How will they hear my script?

JAXTON: They were only going to hear the white half anyway. This would be closer to equal.

CADEN: What do we do, mime the story of the first Thanksgiving?

ALICIA: Mimes are so rude.

JAXTON: I think we just . . . feel the words.

ALICIA: I can do that.

LOGAN: Fine, let's give it a try.

CADEN: No.

LOGAN: Caden, it's a fluid process. It doesn't mean we are abandoning script completely.

CADEN: Yes it does. You've talked yourselves into this equality thing. I have written sixty-two plays for grown-ups and this is the first one that has been read by actors over the age of nine. Do you have any idea how hard it is to labor over every line of historically correct language then only hear them read by people who can't read three-syllable words? It's excruciating. This is finally my chance to have my words read by people who can spell "theater."

ALICIA: It's "R-E" right?

CADEN: That's a very interesting debate that I'll tell you about later. But right now I'm not letting you take away my chance to have my words read by grown-ups.

JAXTON: It's the right thing to do. Go, Alicia.

(Alicia jumps right into sexy Pilgrim poses.)

CADEN: I can't go back to third grade! I won't!

(Jaxton joins Alicia in the silent scene.)

Good Native king and good interpreter!

JAXTON: Respect the math, Caden.

(The following action sequence moves quickly, overlapping lines.)

CADEN: Welcome on this day of—

JAXTON: Shhh.

CADEN: The good Lord's feast of—

JAXTON: Shut it.

CADEN: Thanksgiving.

(Jaxton puts his hand over Caden's mouth to silence him.)

LOGAN: Respectful touch. Respectful touch.
CADEN *(Muffled)*: What may I offer . . .

(Caden escapes Jaxton.)

to make your visit pleasing?

(It becomes a comedic scuffle, two non-fighters. Alicia joins their scuffle, but while being sexy and silent except to interject squeals or concern.)

LOGAN: Alicia, please stop that.
JAXTON: Don't push me, Caden.
CADEN: I, Samoset, request the fowl your men gathered—
LOGAN: Think about the kids!
CADEN: with their exploding sticks! Massasoit, which part of the bird is most pleasing to your countenance? That which is most succulent pleaseth me.
JAXTON: You're ruining the simplicity!
LOGAN: We are the future!
CADEN: The breast is ample—
JAXTON: That's it.

(Jaxton tries to stop Caden one final time.)

CADEN: Whilst the leg is moist!
LOGAN: Everyone just stop doing anything!!

(Everyone freezes in a weird physical moment.
    Once they have settled, Logan notices the empty center of the room.)

We've done it.

JAXTON: This?

LOGAN: In the middle of the room. Look at it.

(Everyone looks.)

CADEN: What?

ALICIA: I don't see it.

LOGAN: That is our play.

CADEN: I'm not following.

LOGAN: That space in the middle. That perfectly equitable emptiness.

ALICIA: I wanna see.

CADEN: The room is the play?

LOGAN: We've been trying too hard. The *empty space* is completely, finally equal. That is our Thanksgiving play.

CADEN: So the entire play is "nothingness"?

ALICIA: Oh, I see *that*.

LOGAN: Four white people can't do a play about Thanksgiving that doesn't piss off the funders or the parents or the universe. So we don't. Feel it for a moment.

(They do.)

ALICIA: I feel it!

CADEN: It is . . . something.

JAXTON: This nothing breaks the cycle of lies, stereotypes, and inequality.

CADEN: The parents can't object to that.

JAXTON: It's brilliant, Lo. You did it.

LOGAN: No, we did it. We all created this nothing together.

(They appreciate their accomplishment.)

JAXTON: So we're done!

CADEN: That's it?

LOGAN: One rehearsal. That's got to be a record.

JAXTON: That's how us professionals roll.

ALICIA: But I think I have a contract to act in a play.

LOGAN: You and Jaxton will still be credited as actors and collaborators. Caden will have an added credit of dramaturg.

(Caden inhales sharply, instantly emotional.)

CADEN: Dramaturg? The holy grail of American theater titles.

ALICIA: What is that?

CADEN: No one knows.

ALICIA: I still get paid for the rest of the rehearsals, right?

LOGAN: Of course.

CADEN: Can we come back tomorrow?

LOGAN: We don't have to. But the space is here for us if we want it.

CADEN: We could work on the sex comedy.

ALICIA: I'd like that.

(She throws her version of a sex comedy into the room.)

LOGAN: As the director I should technically be in the room.

CADEN: So, same time tomorrow? I'll bring pages.

ALICIA: I'll be late. Just . . . because.

CADEN: Because of the bus?

ALICIA: Oh right. That's why.

CADEN: I could give you a ride home. And pick you up. And give you a ride home again.

(Alicia considers him.)

ALICIA: OK. Can you also write a play for me? I want to portray a better-known historical feminist woman like Carrie Bradshaw. Or Lara Croft. Or Shakira.

CADEN: Sure.

(Alicia and Caden go. Quick goodbyes all around.
Logan offers the recoupling gesture. Jaxton joins her.)

LOGAN: Are we OK?

JAXTON: Yeah. You've inspired me, Lo, really.

LOGAN: Thank you. That means a lot.

JAXTON: This piece, the nothing. It's taught me that we need
to do more of that.

LOGAN: How can the play be more than nothing?

JAXTON: Not the play. We need to be less. Do less. That's the
lesson. By doing nothing, we become part of the solution.
But it has to start here, with us.

LOGAN: Yes.

(They appreciate the nothing a moment more.
Lights out.
The center of the room remains lit but empty.)

END OF PLAY

WHAT WOULD CRAZY HORSE DO?

A DARK DRAMEDY INSPIRED BY AN ACTUAL EVENT

PRODUCTION HISTORY

What Would Crazy Horse Do? was first produced by Relative Theatrics (Anne Mason, Founder and Producing Artistic Director; Alex Soto, Production Manager) at Laramie Plains Civic Center's Gryphon Theatre in Laramie, Wyoming, on March 30, 2017. It was directed by Kathryn Demith and Anne Mason. The scenic and prop design were by Sara Pugh, the costume design was by Dee Sullivan, the lighting design was by Cory Hill, the sound design was by John Wilhelm; the dramaturg was Mak Booher and the stage manager was Alexandria Skaar. The cast was:

JOURNEY	Talissa Littlesun
CALVIN	Piram Duran
EVAN	Anne Mason
REBEL	Kevin Inouye

What Would Crazy Horse Do? had its world premiere at Kansas City Repertory Theatre (Eric Rosen, Artistic Director; Angela Lee Gieras, Executive Director; Jerry Genochio, Producing Director) on April 28, 2017. It was directed by Sam Pinkleton. The scenic design was by Antje Ellermann, the costume design was by Gretchen Halle, the lighting design was by Michelle

Harvey, the sound design was by Stowe Nelson; the dramaturg was Dalton Pierce and the production stage manager was April Elizabeth Brewer. The cast was:

JOURNEY	Roseanne Supernault
CALVIN	Christopher Reed Brown
EVAN	Amy Attaway
REBEL	Jason Chanos

CHARACTERS

JOURNEY GOOD EAGLE: Female, Native American, twenty-six, Calvin's twin sister. Usually a bit erratic, going off the deep end since the death of their grandfather. A warrior, not a victim. Reservation accent.

CALVIN GOOD EAGLE: Male, Native American, twenty-six, Journey's twin brother. Educated at Yale. Devoted to his sister but she makes it hard.

EVAN ATWOOD: Female, Caucasian (Anglo looking), thirty to forty-five, first female leader of the Ku Klux Klan. Strong, educated woman on the verge of bringing the Klan into a new era of political influence and power.

REBEL SHAW: Male, Caucasian (Anglo looking), thirty-five to forty-five, Legacy KKK member from the South. Evan's bodyguard but much more. Backwoods Southern accent.

SETTING

Journey and Calvin's home that they lived in with their grandfather. Although they are of the (fictional) Marahotah tribe, they live on a Lakota reservation in South Dakota.

SCENE ONE

Walter Good Eagle's grave. Journey and Calvin, in regalia, kneel in the grass over the grave. Their faces and hands are covered in white paint or makeup.

They perform a traditional ceremony. Suddenly Journey jumps up and frantically wipes at her face and hands, trying to get the white off.

JOURNEY: FUCK!
CALVIN: Journey, what's wrong?
JOURNEY: I can't breathe!

(She violently runs her sleeve across her face.)

CALVIN: You'll hurt yourself.
JOURNEY: Get it off! Get it off!!

(Journey drags her sleeves across her face hard enough to peel skin.)

CALVIN: Calm down.

(Calvin grabs at her arms.)

JOURNEY: Get it the fuck off!

(They struggle. Calvin keeps coming at her, steady and calm.)

Please, brother. Get it off of me.
CALVIN: I will. I'll take care of you.

(Journey relaxes, Calvin uses his sleeve to carefully clean the white off her face.)

You got it all over your eyes. Hold still one sec.

(He grabs his water bottle. A little left. He positions her head and pours it into her eyes.)

JOURNEY: Ow!
CALVIN: Sorry.
JOURNEY: Making it run into my eyes is so much better.

(She uses her own sleeve, carefully this time.)

CALVIN: Fine, do it yourself.
JOURNEY: I am.
CALVIN: I see that.
JOURNEY: You gonna pout now?
CALVIN: I don't pout.
JOURNEY: My brother, you are the King of Pout. You have the certificate to prove it.
CALVIN: You making me a "King of Pout" certificate does not make it true.

JOURNEY: Admit it, you want me to get more shit in my eyes so you can save me, don't you?

CALVIN: No.

JOURNEY: Just a little bit, right?

(They smile.)

CALVIN: Stop it. I want you to feel better. You know that.

JOURNEY: I know.

(She finishes wiping the white off.)

CALVIN: You feel better?

JOURNEY: It felt like it was suffocating me.

CALVIN: A Native American feeling suffocated by whiteness. So. Many. Jokes.

JOURNEY: Don't joke about traditions. At least not funeral ones.

CALVIN: I don't know what to tell you. We've worn this paint a hundred times before.

JOURNEY: More.

CALVIN: Yeah.

JOURNEY: Maybe we did it wrong? We haven't made it alone before.

CALVIN: It's just chalk and water and earth. I watched Grandpa do it every time.

JOURNEY: Can we still finish the ceremony? Without it?

CALVIN: Yes. We just have the last part.

(They return to their previous position and finish the ceremony. They stand and hold hands over the grave.)

JOURNEY: Goodbye, Grandpa.

CALVIN: Goodbye.

JOURNEY: Everything has changed.

CALVIN: I know.

JOURNEY: It's just the two of us.

CALVIN: I know.

JOURNEY: You can't leave me alone. Ever.

CALVIN: Never.

JOURNEY: Promise.

CALVIN: I promise I won't leave you.

JOURNEY: No, we promise we won't leave each other. That neither of us will ever be alone. On Grandpa's grave, right now, we promise.

(Something big is happening between them.)

We have to do it. Before it's too late.

CALVIN: OK. Together forever. I promise.

JOURNEY: Never alone. I promise.

CALVIN: Womb to tomb.

JOURNEY: Womb to tomb.

SCENE TWO

Day. The main room of the Walter Good Eagle house. It belonged to an old man of extremely limited means.

Old mismatched furniture. Piles of things that are no longer useful, but can't be parted with, line the walls. Strewn here and there are feathers, leather medicine bags, dried plants, tobacco, rocks, bits of beading—a collection of gifts to an elder. Native-patterned blankets cover furniture and hang over windows.

The newest items are all funeral-related: old flowers, boxes of food, casserole dishes to be picked up, cards, etc.

Calvin works on his laptop. Journey studies a chessboard across from him.

Outside, Evan and Rebel approach the house. Evan is solid as a rock, Rebel is uncomfortable. They knock.

JOURNEY *(Yelling)*: We don't want any more funeral food!
CALVIN: They're giving it out of respect for Grandpa. Be gracious.

JOURNEY: Screw that. It's death food and I don't want it in our house!

CALVIN *(Calls out)*: One sec. *(To Journey)* Leave the room if you can't control yourself. Someone will have you committed and I'm left alone. I'm serious.

(Calvin pulls himself together and opens the door. Journey studies the chessboard.)

Oh, hello? Can I help you?

EVAN: Evan Atwood. And this is my associate Rebel Shaw. We are looking for Walter Good Eagle.

JOURNEY: Too late.

EVAN: We came a long way for this meeting. When he didn't show at the restaurant I was concerned, but if you're saying he has skipped out on us and—

JOURNEY: He's gone.

REBEL: We have an agreement.

CALVIN: He passed away last week.

(Evan and Rebel make significant eye contact.)

EVAN: Oh. I am so sorry.

CALVIN: What kind of agreement?

EVAN: Were you related to him?

CALVIN: He was our grandfather. You knew him?

EVAN: We've only been in contact recently. Walter knew my grandfather. I think you may be able to help us.

JOURNEY: We're busy.

CALVIN: Stop it. *(To Rebel and Evan)* I'm Calvin and this is my sister, Journey.

JOURNEY: Twin sister.

(Calvin glares at her.)

It makes us exotic.

EVAN: Again, I am so sorry to hear of your loss. My own grandfather passed away before I was born, but I owe my life's work to his legacy.

CALVIN: Our grandfather raised us.

EVAN: That's wonderful.

JOURNEY: Because our parents died.

EVAN: I'm sorry.

JOURNEY: Why, did you kill them?

EVAN: Not that I am aware of. But you never know, do you?

JOURNEY: Fair enough. What do you want?

(Evan pulls a folder out of her bag and hands a photo to Calvin.)

EVAN: This is Walter, correct?

CALVIN: That's his dance regalia, so it must be, but I've never seen a picture of him this young.

(Calvin studies the picture.)

JOURNEY: Where did you get this?

EVAN: That man with Walter is my grandfather.

CALVIN: There's so many Marahotah dancers. Where was this taken?

EVAN: At an event in honor of my grandfather.

JOURNEY: "In honor" of your grandfather? You saying our people were a bunch of dancing monkeys for your white grandfather?

CALVIN: Journey.

EVAN: I misspoke. The event was a celebration of your people and mine. My grandfather was the head of the organization that sponsored this Marahotah powwow so he was a special guest.

JOURNEY: Who are your people? White people? *(Looking to Rebel)* Redneck people?

CALVIN: I'm sorry. She's—

JOURNEY: Don't be sorry for me, brother.

REBEL: I don't need your sorrys either, son.

CALVIN: Ms. Atwood, I'd like to know more about this photo. I am . . . well . . . I'm now the leading expert on our tribe and I've never heard of a powwow of this many Marahotah.

EVAN: There was a unique connection between our grandfathers. Do you recognize this?

(Evan pulls a beaded medallion out of her bag.
Calvin and Journey are visibly struck.
Calvin goes to a closet and pulls out his regalia from the burial ceremony. We see a matching medallion in the center of his shirt.)

CALVIN: Grandpa gave this to me when I became a man.

EVAN: As you can see, there are two of them on his regalia. He gave you one, but after he had given my grandfather the other. Can we come in and explain?

(Journey and Calvin try to take it all in.)

CALVIN: Who was your grandfather?

EVAN: His name was Doctor Evans. He was on the cover of *LIFE* magazine once.

CALVIN: An academic? Did he study our people? *(Indicating medallion)* Are there other pieces like this we don't know about?

(Evan and Rebel decide something. Evan pulls a piece of paper out of the folder.)

I don't understand.

EVAN: It's very clear. That is Walter Good Eagle posing on a flyer for a powwow sponsored by the Ku Klux Klan.

CALVIN: Your grandfather is this Hiram Wesley Evans?

EVAN: Yes. Walter gave his medallion to the Imperial Wizard of the Klan.

JOURNEY: You said he gave you your life's work.

CALVIN: You're affiliated with a man who led the Klan?

REBEL: We are the Klan.

(Silence. Then Calvin and Journey laugh.)

(To Evan) This never happened when we wore the robes.

CALVIN: OK, you had us going. But for real, this isn't funny. Our grandfather died only a week ago and he was a jokester, but this is crossing the line. Who—

EVAN: I regret the unfortunate timing, but this is not a joke. The medallion—

JOURNEY: What he's saying is get the fuck out of our house.

EVAN: I understand your confusion, but I assure you everything we've said is true.

(Evan extends a business card.)

CALVIN: Anyone can make a fake card.

EVAN: Seriously, who makes a Ku Klux Klan business card? I've got hundreds of them.

(Calvin has to wonder.)

CALVIN: What the hell are you doing here?

EVAN: This powwow was a watershed moment for my grandfather that caused him to radically change the doctrine of the Klan and grow it to the largest public numbers in the organization's history, before it was taken over by hate-filled radicals. Today, Rebel and I are poised to relaunch the Klan as a completely different kind of organization, the Free Americans. And your grandfather agreed to help us.

CALVIN: I don't know how you got this medallion and the photo, but you are obviously lying. You need to leave.

(Calvin ushers Evan and Rebel toward the door.)

EVAN: I understand you need time, but we have a signed contract. As an act of good will we paid your grandfather in advance. We have poured an incredible amount of money and marketing into this event.

CALVIN: If this is true, you can have your money back. How much was it?

REBEL: Twenty thousand dollars.

JOURNEY: You're a fucking liar. This is my grandfather's house. He doesn't have that kind of money.

EVAN: Walter received the check.

CALVIN: We'll get to the bottom of it, but he's gone so he won't be able to fulfill the contract. If there is one.

EVAN: A Marahotah will be part of this event. Or are there others we should talk to instead?

CALVIN: Good luck with that.

EVAN: Fine. Keep this copy of the contract for your records. We'll be back.

CALVIN: You're serious.

EVAN: Absolutely.

JOURNEY: Get the fuck out!

(Journey rushes toward them. Rebel jumps in front of Evan, ready to take Journey on.)

REBEL: Show some respect, girl.

EVAN: Rebel, stand down. We're going. But we'll be back. Look into the information. It's all true.

(They go.)

JOURNEY: What the fuck was that?

CALVIN: Bullshit. Total bullshit . . . Right?

JOURNEY: Of course. This is our grandfather we're talking about. He taught us everything about the Marahotah ways. He didn't make some deal with the wannabe KKK to buy a boat.

CALVIN: A boat? In the middle of the prairie?

JOURNEY: I don't know. Something that costs a lot of money.

CALVIN: This is his signature. I'd know it anywhere.

JOURNEY: It's a lie. All of it.

CALVIN: Of course.

JOURNEY: What about the twin pact?

CALVIN: There's no such thing as a "twin pact." You made that up.

JOURNEY: Whatever you call it, we have a plan. Maybe this is a sign we should do it now.

CALVIN: When we leave this world it needs to mean something. Make a statement.

JOURNEY: Our tribe going extinct via double suicide is a pretty strong message.

CALVIN: Not if no one hears it.

JOURNEY: You are changing your mind about this.

CALVIN: I promised on Grandpa's grave, we'll never be alone. But I need more time to make a plan.

JOURNEY: Fine. But don't stall until it's too late, brother.

CALVIN: I'm not stalling. Thanks to us, the Marahotah will finally mean something to the world.

SCENE THREE

A week later, midday. Journey sorts the mail. She's in a really good mood.

JOURNEY: There's something from the bank. And my package!

(Calvin, sullen, takes and rips open an envelope, as Journey excitedly opens the package.)

CALVIN: Finally. Can't just give me the account information. Have to verify his death and mail it.

(He adds the letter to a paper-clipped bunch.)

JOURNEY: You're such a whiner. What does it say? Is it Grandpa's secret account? Does it have millions in it?

CALVIN: Nope. And that's the last account I could track down on him. Unless he buried the money in the yard, there isn't any.

JOURNEY: Bummer.

CALVIN: That's good news.

JOURNEY: No, this is . . . Ta-da!

(*She unfurls a banner that reads "What Would Crazy Horse Do?"*)

CALVIN: What's that for?

JOURNEY: I ordered it online to cheer you up. You've been so mopey.

(*She gets on a chair to hang it from one side of the room. Calvin helps her.*)

Catchy, isn't it?

CALVIN: But what's the point?

JOURNEY: You've spent two years doing that paper thingy on Crazy Horse. You love him. You'd be his stalker.

CALVIN: My *dissertation* is a serious comparison of celebrity and leadership today against the nearly invisible, reluctant leadership style of Crazy Horse. In this age of social media and the NSA—

JOURNEY: "What Would Crazy Horse Do?" is perfect. WWCHD leather bracelets will become a worldwide meme for social justice and noncompliance with the invaders. A meme for saying: "Screw you," and doing whatever is necessary to rise up, resist, and survive!

CALVIN: Or die.

JOURNEY: Fuck them either way. But when they find us, they'll see this and be all: "What the hell?" They'll totally put it in the paper, and people will Google it and order lots of bracelets. Crazy Horse everywhere!

CALVIN: Bracelets from whom? We'll be gone.

JOURNEY: I can set something up. The point is, Crazy Horse will live on because of us! And all the stuff he did.

CALVIN: He's Lakota not Marahotah.

JOURNEY: We live on their reservation. We may as well be Lakota.

CALVIN: But we're not.

JOURNEY: You always say we need to make a statement with our lives. Done. Yay!

(Calvin goes back to sorting papers in the box.)

CALVIN: I'm a little busy organizing ten years of Grandpa's mail while you're designing banners on my computer that you didn't ask to use.

JOURNEY: Oh my God. Last year you complained that I'm not doing anything. Now I do shit and you still complain. I knew your time at Yale would change you, but I didn't think we'd never be us again.

CALVIN: We nearly have the same DNA. We can't be more us.

JOURNEY: Maybe Crazy Horse was right to stay away from the white people. They can steal your soul.

CALVIN: Yale did not steal my soul. Crushed it a little, but that was bound to happen eventually.

JOURNEY: It's more than that.

CALVIN: You want to talk about change? You were a basket case last year.

JOURNEY: Don't be dramatic.

CALVIN: Grandpa and I thought we were going to lose you.

JOURNEY: Well, I'm still here.

CALVIN: And just when I think I can work on my paper again, Grandpa dies and you . . . do what you did.

JOURNEY: It was a natural reaction.

CALVIN: It wasn't.

JOURNEY: I'm fine now.

CALVIN: Yeah, right. Just don't accuse me of being the one who changed.

(Journey turns and admires her banner.)

JOURNEY: I like it. But I guess it should be a Marahotah leader instead of Crazy Horse. In case it gets in the paper.

CALVIN: It's OK to admire Crazy Horse.

(Calvin reads a letter or email.)

Shit. From the State History Museum. A copy of the original Klan flyer—and there's Grandpa.

(He holds up a copy of Evan's KKK flyer.)

But if they didn't pay him, the contract is breached and we're done with that part of the bullshit.

JOURNEY: Good. When they get here we kick them to the curb. If we had one.

CALVIN: But we can't let that woman use the flyer to smear Grandpa's memory.

JOURNEY: We could shoot both of them when they walk in. Problem solved.

CALVIN: Ha ha. You know I don't believe in violence.

JOURNEY: That's awesome, brother. You may not believe in violence, but it sure as hell believes in you. Tell me the truth. In our situation with Klan lady, what *would* Crazy Horse do?

CALVIN: Probably the shooting thing.

JOURNEY: There you go.

CALVIN: Don't joke.

JOURNEY: I'm not.

(A knock. Calvin opens the door. Evan and Rebel.)

EVAN: Remember me?

JOURNEY: Nope.

CALVIN: Come in.

(Calvin extends his hand. Evan hesitates, then extends hers. Calvin suddenly doesn't want to take it. They both drop their hands.)

EVAN: So, did you do your research? Do you believe we are telling the truth?

CALVIN: I believe you did not make up the flyer. Beyond that, I'm not sure what to believe.

EVAN: We are sincere. The Ku Klux Klan is holding a commemorative powwow and we need you to be in it.

(Journey grabs the flyer.)

JOURNEY: You know you can't just put a "K" in front of things and turn it Klan. I mean look at this thing. "The South Dakota Klavern invites you to a Kar" K-A-R "Klassic." K-L-A. "PopKorn will be served." They put a fucking K in the middle of popcorn.

EVAN: It was a big event. They may have overdone it a bit.

JOURNEY: And topping it all off, a Klan powwow. "With original American Indians for your entertainment."

EVAN: This event will celebrate the coming together of our people in a new era of understanding.

The way Dr. Evans envisioned before our organization was corrupted by hate.

CALVIN: Technically, you are a hate group.

EVAN: Our group is about racial pride, in the exact same way you take pride in your culture.

CALVIN: You're proud of the culture of whiteness?

EVAN: Basically.

JOURNEY: What exactly does "cultural whiteness" look like?

EVAN: George Washington.

REBEL: And nearly all of the presidents.

EVAN: Walt Disney, Shania Twain.

JOURNEY: Adolf Hitler.

EVAN: Funny. But the truth is, we do not hate anyone.

JOURNEY: I hate *lots* of people.

EVAN: I am sorry to hear that because there is another way to live.

JOURNEY: Bullshit.

EVAN: Our organization does not condone profanity, drink alcohol to excess, or use drugs.

JOURNEY: I think she just called me a foul-mouthed, drunk Indian.

EVAN: I am pointing out that there are positives to our organization we can all agree on. There is a reason Dr. Evans grew us to four million public members and countless more.

CALVIN: I've looked into this contract—

EVAN: Come on, Calvin, our people and your people have never had seriously strained relations.

JOURNEY: Your people killed millions of our people.

EVAN: I mean the Klan specifically. And according to this history, we had good relations at one point. We want to honor and explore that history.

JOURNEY: By making us their token Indians.

EVAN: By giving you a platform. Think about it, few groups have a stronger romanticized image than the Ku Klux Klan and Native Americans. Put us together for one day, and the whole world will tune in to watch. Our marketing machine is prepared to get every social media outlet, news network, and Indian-loving German tuned into this event.

CALVIN: You can do that? That kind of coverage?

JOURNEY: Coverage of the Klan parading behind us in a bunch of hoods.

EVAN: We are no longer an invisible organization. The Free Americans stand proud, without hoods. And we are offering you full autonomy in the press. We bring them to you and you say whatever you want, alone.

CALVIN: Wait. You mean that? You'd let us say anything we want?

EVAN: Absolutely.

CALVIN: Are you really going to do this? As big as you say?

EVAN: Our followers are mobilizing from every state and ten countries around the world. Our message will sweep across this nation and beyond.

CALVIN: Huh. If we did this—

JOURNEY: That's enough. *(To Evan)* Get out!

(Journey puts herself between Calvin and Evan.)

CALVIN: What my sister means to say is that we have to discuss this privately.

JOURNEY: No, we don't.

EVAN: We'll wait outside.

JOURNEY: Don't wait.

(Evan and Rebel duck out.)

I better hear your car starting!

CALVIN: Calm down.

JOURNEY: You calm down. You aren't considering this, are you?

CALVIN: Look, I'm committed to the twin pact thing, but if we want it to send a message for our people—

JOURNEY: The memory of our people.

CALVIN: Whatever. I don't think that's something we can pull off by ourselves.

JOURNEY: So your plan is to partner with the Klan?

CALVIN: Think about it. If we don't join them, we've made a bad enemy. But, if we say what we want to and decide to kill ourselves right in the middle of their powwow, with all that news coverage, we're martyrs. Better yet, we're Native American Indians who took on the Klan martyrs.

JOURNEY: The Klan will hijack our story and the Marahotah won't be remembered at all. We agreed to make our deaths do something, brother.

CALVIN: We'll mess up the Klan on national TV. I'll be on national TV. Maybe international. This is so much better than Crazy Horse bracelets.

JOURNEY: Why do you trust these guys? If they find out what you're planning we'll be back to nothing, maybe worse.

CALVIN: Crazy Horse single-handedly terrorized the gold miners in the Black Hills. He saw a way that a solitary man could move among the miners unseen and made the United States think twice about panning for gold in Indian land. I believe I can be that man with these guys before I'm done.

JOURNEY: *"I'm done"*?

CALVIN: We're done.

JOURNEY: Crazy Horse failed. All the gold's gone.

CALVIN: He never lived among them, so he didn't understand them like I do. History loves a scandal. I want to do this.

(Journey studies her brother.)

JOURNEY: I can see that. Get her back inside.

(Calvin goes to get Evan. Journey goes to the desk and opens a drawer.)

Crazy Horse killed his people's horses rather than let them surrender to the reservations. This is what Crazy Horse would do.

(As soon as Evan enters Journey aims a gun at her.)

CALVIN: No!

(Calvin jumps in front of Journey. Evan ducks for cover. Journey fires.

    Evan and Calvin's shoulders jerk back, dropping them both to the floor.)

JOURNEY: CALVIN!

(She rushes to him. He sits up.)

Are you OK?
CALVIN: It grazed me. I'm fine.
JOURNEY: Oh my God! I'm so sorry!
CALVIN: You can't keep doing shit like this!

(Evan groans. Journey lifts the gun again. Calvin grabs it from her.

    Evan sits up, holding her shoulder. A red stain spreads through her clothes.)

Oh my God.

(Calvin rushes to help Evan. She pulls away.)

EVAN: Don't touch me.
CALVIN: I won't hurt you. You have to understand this isn't her fault. My sister isn't right in her head. She's been through tragedy and—
EVAN: I'm fine.
CALVIN: You know you've been shot.
EVAN: Not the first time.

(Rebel crashes through the door, gun drawn. Calvin instinctively pulls Journey's gun. Rebel swings toward him. Journey throws herself on Calvin.)

Stop! Put the gun down, Rebel.

(Rebel focuses on Evan. He's visibly upset. He rushes to her, gun still in his hand.)

REBEL: I go for one smoke! —I'll quit the things tonight. Shit.
EVAN: It's just a shoulder, no cause for profanity.

(Rebel rips right into her clothes, triage style.)

CALVIN *(To Journey)*: What if he had shot you? You would have left me alone.
JOURNEY: I'm sorry. I felt like she was taking you away from me.
CALVIN: We're together in this. Do you hear me?
JOURNEY: Yes.
REBEL: I need some towels, something to disinfect the wound, and my bag from the car.
CALVIN: You're not taking her to a doctor?
EVAN: Don't be stupid. Gunshot wounds are reported to the police. My organization is not coming into the light unless it is in the way I have orchestrated.
CALVIN: OK. Good.
REBEL: The supplies, now! I'm not leaving her alone with you igits.
CALVIN: Journey, get a towel.
JOURNEY: Fuck that.
CALVIN: Really? You shoot someone in our house, she's not calling the police, and you're gonna be a shit about it?

(Journey goes. Rebel tosses keys to Calvin. He goes.)

REBEL: I'll get you stabilized, then we're out of here.

EVAN: You know that if the wolves in our organization smell blood, it is all they need to rise up, scare the sheep, and we're out. Or worse.

REBEL: It doesn't have to be the Klan. We could start another organization—

EVAN: 2042 is closer every day. Because of our work, the Klan is the only organization prepared to fight the genocide of the white race.

REBEL: Does it have to be the powwow, with this crazy squaw?

(Journey returns with towels.)

EVAN: This new event with these two will not only bring Free Americans press, but *good* press. And that's something we have not been able to buy for over eighty years.

REBEL: Where I come from, you see a rabid dog, you put it down. Not that I would. Just saying.

EVAN: You won't need the gun. Journey is going to be fine.

(Calvin returns and gives Rebel the bag. Rebel tends to Evan's wound, keeping the gun handy. Evan stays solid.)

Since we're all here now, we should discuss the event.

JOURNEY: You're fucking kidding me.

EVAN: We came with a job to do, and we're going to do it.

CALVIN: I don't think—

EVAN: But I do. Especially now. You are appearing at that pow-wow. Think it out, Calvin.

CALVIN: If we don't, you call the police on Journey.

JOURNEY: They just said they don't want the police involved.

EVAN: If that is my only choice to get you to cooperate, I will take it.

JOURNEY: Do it, lady.

CALVIN: I don't think she's bluffing.

JOURNEY: Me neither.

CALVIN: Do you want us to be separated?

JOURNEY: I won't dance for these people.

EVAN: And then there's the money issue.

JOURNEY: There wasn't any. We checked.

EVAN: Wrong.

(Rebel pulls out a sheet of paper and gives it to Calvin.)

CALVIN: He signed the check over to my student loans? That's not possible. I would have known.

EVAN: It didn't go through. He didn't have your loan information right. But we corrected that. You'll see it credited on your next statement. So, that's our end of the contract fulfilled.

REBEL: Thought you guys went to school for free.

JOURNEY: Yeah, Yale comes with our fantastic free health care.

REBEL: I know a lot of folks who would kill for some free government health care.

JOURNEY: Have you ever been to an Indian Health Services clinic?

REBEL: Gotta be better than nothing.

JOURNEY: Yeah, because there's nothing more reliable than a government-run agency. Nothing more safe. Shit, the same good liberals who believe the U.S. government conspired to bomb the Twin Towers are fighting to hand their lives over to that government in the form of socialized health care. People are fucking idiots.

EVAN: Calvin, you decide which way you want to go with this. We either charge Journey with attempted murder or we do this event and everyone wins.

CALVIN: You don't have to threaten us. We're in.

EVAN: Great. Let's talk about the powwow. We want to be sure we treat your beliefs with the utmost respect and propriety. How would you like to be addressed: Native American or American Indian?

REBEL: Oh my Gawd.   JOURNEY: You're fucking
                                        kidding me.

CALVIN: Journey and I are members of the Marahotah Tribe. That's our word for ourselves.

EVAN: Thank you.

JOURNEY (*To Rebel*): How about you? What do you like to be called? Nazi? Skinhead? Redneck?

REBEL: My title is Grand Giant.

(*Journey bursts out laughing.*)

JOURNEY: Seriously?

REBEL: Shut up, squaw.

JOURNEY: Dick.

REBEL: Pussy.

EVAN: Rebel, language.

CALVIN (*To Evan*): What are you called?

EVAN: My title is Imperial Dragon.

CALVIN: Isn't that the president of the Klan?

EVAN: More like vice president.

REBEL: For now.

JOURNEY: So if I was a better shot, I would have done the world a big favor?

CALVIN: Be quiet and let me handle this.

JOURNEY: Right, because we're best buds with the Ku Klux Klan now. And the whole world's gonna see it.

CALVIN: Stop it.

JOURNEY: Fuck that. I say we stick to the pact and be done with it before things get any worse.

(Journey takes the gun and caresses it. Rebel pulls his gun, just in case.)

CALVIN: Give it back, Journey.

JOURNEY: I see how people get hooked on shooting these things. It feels so good.

REBEL: Girl, I'm not giving you another chance to shoot at us.

JOURNEY: I'm not interested in either of you.

CALVIN: Stop.

JOURNEY: We're doing it anyway, Calvin, and like dragon lady said, "We're screwed." Let's be done.

CALVIN: Don't you dare go crazy on me again.

JOURNEY: It's not crazy. We promised.

CALVIN: Not like this. No one will remember like this. Don't let it be like Willow. Or Marianna. Or Vincent.

JOURNEY: Or Martin.

CALVIN: Joseph.

JOURNEY: Neil.

CALVIN: No one remembers them.

JOURNEY: No one but us.

CALVIN: If you do it like this, no one will remember the Marahotah at all.

JOURNEY: Neil watched three of his friends blow their brains out, then still had the courage to pull the trigger, all alone. Can you imagine that? I try to all the time.

(Journey pictures it. Calvin gets scared.)

CALVIN: Journey. Come back to me.

JOURNEY: No one would have known if he didn't do it, but he made a promise and he fucking followed through.

CALVIN: What about the twin pact?

JOURNEY: You don't believe in it.

CALVIN: Of course I do.

JOURNEY: You're never going to do it, are you? You're going to let me go alone.

CALVIN: If we do it, we do it together.

JOURNEY: If? My sweet brother. You know the chances are that we won't go exactly together.

CALVIN: You don't know that. If we plan it right . . . we came into this world together, we can leave it the same. Womb to tomb.

JOURNEY: Womb to tomb.

(Journey sets the gun down.)

EVAN: Who were those people?

CALVIN: Friends who have committed suicide. The most recent ones.

JOURNEY: The last four count as one. Four kids took one gun and drew cards. Low card won and got to shoot himself first. The highest card went last.

REBEL: Shit.

EVAN: You'd think we'd hear about four suicides on the news.

JOURNEY: Turns out colonization is a perfect system. When you all stopped killing us, you got us to do it ourselves.

EVAN: You have to believe me, we're not here to ruin your life.

JOURNEY: I really don't have to believe anything you say.

EVAN: What is your ideal world, Journey? How about one free of the white race? A world where your people live together and have children together and learn your culture completely free and clear of everyone else?

JOURNEY: We had that once.

EVAN: That is the dream of our organization. We do not want to abolish races, we simply want them to be allowed to live separately, as God intended. Whites with whites, Indians with Indians. Each race becoming clean and pure as they were meant to be. Imagine, a few generations from now, an entire race of full-blooded Marahotah, like it was before everything went bad.

JOURNEY: That's not going to happen, no matter how long you wait.

EVAN: It's biology.

JOURNEY: Calvin and I are the last Marahotah on the face of the earth. Shit, the world rallies to save frogs, but a race of people disappears and no one knows. We didn't—until a couple years ago.

REBEL: There's gotta be others somewhere.

CALVIN: The only ones that may be left are so mixed they wouldn't even call themselves Cherokee.

REBEL: Then shouldn't you be in a museum or something?

JOURNEY: Become Ishi? Become Crazy Horse? They turned themselves over to a white institution and it killed them both.

REBEL: Not to live there. Jeez, that'd kill anybody. But so they record your culture and stuff.

JOURNEY: For who? A bunch of white people running around speaking our language in a feather headdress. It's over. The Marahotah are done. Shouldn't you be happy about this?

REBEL: No. If we let people screw around any way they please, one day we'll be one big brown family across the globe. But is that really what people want? No more white and black and Mexican and Marahotah? No more differences? But you try to point that out and they call you a racist.

If there's one thing you people have taught us, it's that extinction is a real and present danger. Think of how many tribes were wiped out in the ten years after Columbus landed.

EVAN: Your story is at the core of what Rebel and I have been trying to build for the last decade. That future I spoke about can save us all. People don't believe in racial extinction, but you are living proof. Tell your story. Save another tribe before it's too late.

(Journey and Calvin take it in for a moment. Journey shakes herself out of it.)

JOURNEY: You're good, lady. You nearly sucked both of us in in one night. Whitewash your "organization" all you want, but it's still the Klan.

EVAN: Much like the Native Americans, we've been portrayed inaccurately for hundreds of years.

CALVIN: What about the lynching, and terrorizing people for the color of their skin?

EVAN: Fringe lunatics.

JOURNEY: It's not polite to talk about Rebel right in front of him.

REBEL: Don't speak for me, girl.

EVAN: Rebel has proven himself above the stereotypes of his Southern roots. He's quite decorous when you get to know him.

CALVIN: It's easy to say that now, but there seemed to be a lot of people in hoods standing around those lunatics.

EVAN: As easy as it is to dismiss the Natives that attacked and burned wagon trains of women and children?

JOURNEY: That was self-defense.

EVAN: Speaking of shooting defenseless women, another towel please.

(Journey leaves the room.)

I'm worried about her, Calvin.

CALVIN: She's fine.

REBEL: Has she been diagnosed?

CALVIN: For what?

EVAN: She's clearly unstable.

CALVIN: Grandpa's death . . . opened something in her. But I've gotten her through stuff before.

EVAN: Stuff like shooting people?

CALVIN: Not guns . . .

REBEL: But violence, right?

EVAN: She could have killed either of us.

CALVIN: But she didn't.

REBEL: Yet.

> *(Journey returns and tosses a towel at Rebel. Calvin studies her. Rebel inspects the wound.)*

I think the bleeding's stopped enough to stitch it.

EVAN: I'm ready.

> *(Rebel stitches Evan's wound. Evan cringes, but keeps herself together.*
> *Calvin looks away. Journey watches, impressed.)*

CALVIN: You want an . . . asprin or something?

REBEL: I'll have a painkiller and antibiotics called in to the local pharmacy.

CALVIN: We only have an IHS clinic here.

> *(Rebel glares at him.)*

JOURNEY: Don't you listen? The fantastic Indian Health Services. They don't treat white people.

REBEL: You only help your own, and you call us racist?

JOURNEY: YOUR government only subjects Indians to their shitty care.

REBEL: Then I take Calvin to the emergency room. We make up a story about his arm wound and—

CALVIN: The government closed our emergency room last year.

REBEL: So we go to another one.

CALVIN: It was the only one.

REBEL: That doesn't make any sense.

JOURNEY: They realized that the rate of death at the IHS ER was higher than the rate of death if you have to drive eighty miles to the ER off the reservation.

(Rebel is out of ideas.)

EVAN: Calvin, do you have any doctor friends at the IHS clinic that would help us? Discreetly.

CALVIN: There's a nurse I know who may slip us a sample or two. Of antibiotics anyway.

JOURNEY: Who?

CALVIN: She's new.

REBEL: Go get 'em.

CALVIN: We're not leaving you two here, in our home.

JOURNEY: Do I know her?

CALVIN: No.

REBEL: If anyone sees Evan's wound, they'll call the cops.

CALVIN: We can put a jacket on her.

REBEL: I don't want to move her until she has antibiotics. Risking an infection.

CALVIN: Again, we're not leaving you here.

REBEL: Then one of you go alone.

CALVIN: Journey and I stay together.

JOURNEY: How do you know this nurse?

CALVIN: I used to go out, see other people besides you.

REBEL: You some kind of creepy siblings?

JOURNEY: If we were, we would have a baby and keep the tribe going.

CALVIN: Why do you say stuff like that?

JOURNEY: It's a joke.

REBEL: Calvin has to go. He knows the nurse.

JOURNEY: Pretty well, apparently.

CALVIN: Drop it. I'm not leaving you alone with them.

EVAN: Rebel and Calvin go, I'll stay with Journey.

REBEL: Hell no. Calvin goes alone.

CALVIN: I told you, I'm not leaving Journey alone with—	REBEL: I told you, I'm not leaving Evan alone with either of—

JOURNEY: Oh my fucking God! Fine.

(She grabs the gun. Rebel jumps up. Journey hands it to Evan.)

Now she can shoot me if she wants. Go get her the medication before she gets infected and we're stuck with this bitch.

EVAN: Go Rebel.

CALVIN *(To Journey)*: Don't you care that Rebel has a gun and I don't?

JOURNEY: Say hi to your nurse friend for me.

CALVIN: Seriously, will you be OK?

JOURNEY: If we're sticking around, we're gonna have to be apart sometime. Rebel will keep you safe.

(Both Rebel and Calvin look surprised.)

They need us. *(To Rebel)* If anything happens to him, I'll rip her throat out.

REBEL: We'll be right back.

(She and Calvin hug fiercely.)

CALVIN: It's just a trip to town.

JOURNEY: Yup. Done a million of them.

(She finally lets go.)

CALVIN: I don't think you're ready for this.

JOURNEY: It's been two weeks since the accident. We can't stay attached forever.

CALVIN: But if anything happens to you . . .

JOURNEY: Nothing can happen to me without you. We made a pact. Don't forget it.

CALVIN: Not just any pact, a twin pact.

EVAN: We'll be fine.

(Calvin and Rebel go. Journey is clearly upset.)

I've heard twins are close, but you two really are.

JOURNEY: We always were, but there's something about being the last two on the planet.

(Journey watches out the window.)

EVAN: Rebel has an array of military training.

JOURNEY: Some of the drunk drivers on that road have thirty years under their belts.

EVAN: Oh, that's right. That's how Walter died, isn't it?

JOURNEY: On that same road. Driving to town.

EVAN: Tell me about your grandfather.

JOURNEY: He raised us since we were ten. Which is why . . . I thought I knew him.

EVAN: I thought I knew my grandfather too. I was born into the Klan. It was more underground then, but I still grew up in the KKK Kiddies and the Triple K Teen Klub. When I found these pictures of the powwow it seemed to go against everything we stood for. Then I went back and reread every speech my grandfather gave. It was all there, plain as day. I was Klan before, but after that it was different. It became a passion. A true vision. I used my name and worked my way up to become the highest ranking woman in the history of the organization. In the past ten years we've done— We've accomplished a lot, behind the scenes.

JOURNEY: Like what?

EVAN: Just things to pave the way.

JOURNEY: For a powwow?

EVAN: For the glorious reemergence of the public Klan, free of the hate speech and violence-lovers of the past.

JOURNEY: Free of violence? You're calling Rebel harmless?

EVAN: No, he's willing to do what has to be done, but only if it has to be done. Not for love of it, trust me. I wouldn't call you harmless either.

JOURNEY: Lately I've been thinking about the difference between dangerous and effective. I can sit here in the middle of nowhere, ready to pull the trigger, but if no one walks by . . .

EVAN: Does a gun going off in the prairie make a sound if no one is there to hear it?

JOURNEY: Around here guns have been going off for years. Calvin needs to believe that no one heard them because if they have, it means they just don't care.

EVAN: Lucky you, people walked right into your line of fire this time.

JOURNEY: Yeah. This isn't what I imagined, but everything's been bizarre lately.

EVAN: This is actually *not* the strangest night of my life.

JOURNEY: I don't know who's crazier right now, you or me.

EVAN: I think we're a couple of women trying to find our way in unbelievably difficult situations.

JOURNEY: But you actually think this will work. You'll have your powwow with your press conference and we'll be a cautionary tale, and everyone will love the Klan.

EVAN: When you put it that way, it does sound crazy.

JOURNEY: That's the way it is, Evan.

EVAN: People are scared. This world of virtual connectedness makes people feel more isolated than they've ever been. They need to be part of something that tells them they are amazing and perfect just as God made them. They want to know there is a path to true peace on this earth.

JOURNEY: Peace through racial separation?

EVAN: "Each nation has its own God-given qualities, but each can do its own work only if the racial and group qualities are preserved relatively pure. If any nation is mongrelized, that nation will lose its distinctive quality and its power to contribute to civilization." Dr. Evans wrote that the week after he met Walter. Can you honestly tell me Walter didn't think your people were special? That he didn't believe your blood should be preserved in order to enrich mankind?

JOURNEY: Of course he did.

EVAN: That's why Walter agreed to help us after all these years. We're fighting for the same thing. Other races have realized that. The Klan has had African-American chapters since the beginning.

JOURNEY: Really?

EVAN: It's just facts, Journey.

JOURNEY (Shakes herself out of it): Stop fucking with my mind.

EVAN: Honest facts.

JOURNEY: You aren't what I expected.

EVAN: Then the mind f-word is working.

JOURNEY: "F-word"? Seriously?

EVAN: No swearing.

JOURNEY: Come on. It's not swearing, it's a vulgarism. Try it.

EVAN: No thank you.

JOURNEY: If you're gonna fuck my mind, you at least gotta say it.

EVAN: I'd rather not.

JOURNEY: I think you rather would. Come on. It feels good.

EVAN: You have been mind-fucked.

JOURNEY: Nice.

EVAN: Don't tell Rebel I said that.

JOURNEY: Feels good through, right?

EVAN: Lots of things feel good, but that doesn't make them right.

JOURNEY: Lots of things feel pretty fucked-up and we do them too.

EVAN: Are you and Calvin really planning to kill yourselves?

JOURNEY: Um . . . yeah. Some day.

EVAN: It's such a waste.

JOURNEY: We first talked about it when we were ten and lost our parents, but over the years the idea always comes back. Long ago our people dispersed to various reservations and white cities, and started intermarrying. One day we woke up and everyone was gone but the three of us. Then there were two. And those two are fucked by inevitability. My brother and I live on a knife edge cutting through us slowly, draining Marahotah blood from the planet day by day. Any moment that knife could come up and slice us in half.

But we won't let that happen. There won't be any Last of the Marahotahs. At Grandpa's funeral ceremony we promised we'd go out together. Not one sad, lonely Indian, but a tribe for eternity.

EVAN: With that story, you could change the world.

JOURNEY: You can tell it when we're dead.

EVAN: And when will that be?

(Rebel rushes in, carrying a Super Big Gulp.)

JOURNEY: That was fast.

REBEL: Calvin got arrested.

JOURNEY: What the hell did you do?

REBEL: I was sitting in the dam—darn—car outside the clinic, which is shit by the way, and all these people are led out in handcuffs. Doctors, Indians, everything.

JOURNEY: The tribal police know Calvin. They wouldn't—

REBEL: It was the feds.

JOURNEY: Feds? Are you sure?

REBEL: The local cops were real chatty about it on the police scanner. A prescription-drug raid.

JOURNEY: Where'd they take him?

REBEL: How the heck do I know? We've gotta get gone.

EVAN: If they were interested in us they would be here by now.

REBEL: They'll be looking to question us as soon as Calvin tells them to.

JOURNEY: He's not a rat.

REBEL: I could break him in two minutes.

JOURNEY: I need Calvin back. Everything gets wrong when he leaves.

REBEL: We should go.

EVAN: Perhaps.

JOURNEY: No.

(Journey dives for Evan and grabs the gun. She holds it on her as Rebel draws on Journey.)

REBEL: Drop it.

JOURNEY: No one leaves. No one does anything until Calvin gets back.

EVAN: Journey, Calvin may not be back for a long time.

JOURNEY: So? You try to leave and I'll shoot you. And this time Calvin won't be in the way.

REBEL: I'm shooting on three. One—

JOURNEY: I'll shoot on two. Then where the fuck will your organization be?

EVAN: Look. It's the three of us now, so we need to lower the guns and work this out.

JOURNEY: Fuck that. We wait until Calvin comes back.

EVAN: OK, but I'm more likely to keep Rebel awake to shoot you than the other way around.

Come on, Journey, I know it's hard when Calvin leaves you. Let's talk about it.

JOURNEY: I'm not saying shit until Calvin gets here.

REBEL: Screw this. Let me shoot her.

JOURNEY: Just try it.

EVAN: Journey, truth is, Rebel can shoot you through your brainstem and have you on the ground before your finger can react. But that's not what we want here. Lower your gun and we'll talk.

(Rebel smiles. Journey is coming apart.)

JOURNEY: No. You'll go and I'll be alone.

EVAN: You really haven't been alone since Walter died? Tell me about that.

JOURNEY: Shit. I need Calvin.

EVAN: But Calvin isn't coming back tonight.

JOURNEY: Why not?

EVAN: It's the federal government. He'll be in a federal prison so far far away that you'll never see him again. We are all you have left.

JOURNEY: No more mind-fuck talking. Shut your mouth!

(Rebel sights Journey's head.)

REBEL: Bang. You're dead.

JOURNEY: Shut! Up!

> *(Journey clicks music on a computer. Powwow music blares.
> The drumbeats annoy Rebel, but soothe Journey.*
>
> *Evan, Journey and Rebel settle in, guns pointed, and wait.
> Rebel takes a long drink from his cup.)*

SCENE FOUR

Later. Sunset colors the light. The powwow music pounds on. Every-one is tired, but Journey has calmed.

REBEL: I can't take any more of this jungle music! Let me shoot her.

EVAN: His job is to protect my life. Eventually he will kill you and there's nothing I can do.

JOURNEY: I said no talking!

(She cranks the music louder.)

REBEL *(Singing at the top of his lungs)*: "Rocky top, you'll always be, home sweet home to me! Good old Rocky Top, Rocky Top, Tennessee! Rocky Top, Tenne—"

JOURNEY: OK. OK.

(Journey stops the music.)

REBEL: Worse than Guantánamo.

JOURNEY: Shut up or the music comes back.

(Rebel sucks on his drink, empty. He sinks into a sulky silence. Journey does the same.)

EVAN: You know what I've always wondered?

(Journey glares at her.)

What made Walter agree to dance in the original pow-wow in the first place? Let's be honest, the usual reaction to a request from the Klan is . . . yours. Do you have any idea why he did it?

JOURNEY: No.

EVAN: You knew him best. Why would a man like Walter agree to honor my grandfather?

JOURNEY: He didn't care about your grandfather. I'm sure some white guy had to put on this big event and needed help with entertainment. Everyone knew my grandfather was a sucker for that small-town neighbor crap.

EVAN: But it was more than dancing and singing for entertainment. Walter gave that medallion to my grandfather. It must have meaning.

(Journey realizes something.)

JOURNEY: Oh my God.

REBEL: That's it. I can't hold it anymore.

JOURNEY: The bathroom is in the back.

(She focuses her gun on Evan.)

REBEL: I'm not going anywhere.

(He's in pain.)

JOURNEY: I love it. The Grand Giant is taken down by a Super
    Big Gulp.

REBEL: I'm not going down.

JOURNEY: Gosh, I think I hear rain. Or is that a flowing foun-
    tain? Water in a river—

(He cringes.)

REBEL: I'm pissing on the floor.

(He opens his fly clumsily while keeping his gun on Journey.)

JOURNEY: Don't pee on my floor. That's sick.

REBEL: Can't hold it.

*(Rebel faces the wall and a stream of piss comes out. Both women
wince.)*

JOURNEY: What the hell?!?

EVAN: Rebel Shaw!

JOURNEY: Fine! Pee truce. Just stop!

REBEL: Too late. Can't stop.

(Journey lowers her gun.)

JOURNEY: Forget it. Shoot me.

*(She grabs a water bottle and comes at Rebel. She sprays him
and his pee stain with water.
    Rebel jumps back.)*

REBEL: Hey! Watch it.

JOURNEY: Are you kidding me? You just pissed on my wall! You're a fucking animal.

REBEL: You're a fucking idiot.

(Rebel grabs her gun and now holds both on Journey.)

JOURNEY: I don't care. Just zip first. I'm not having that be my last sight on this earth.

EVAN: Agreed.

(He zips.)

REBEL: Sit there, where I can keep an eye on you.

JOURNEY: I'm not sitting by the pissy wall.

REBEL: Fine, sit over there.

(Journey sits across from them.)

Seriously, why we haven't wiped you people off the face of the earth—

EVAN: That's not our goal.

REBEL: But natural selection should have run its course by now. We should get going.

EVAN: Let me check with our federal contact first. See if they know what's happening.

(She texts on her phone while Rebel and Journey stare at each other. Rebel looks at the chess set.)

REBEL: White's gonna lose big time.

JOURNEY: Yeah.

REBEL: You know that?

JOURNEY: White's Calvin.

REBEL: Thought he was the Yale genius.

JOURNEY: It takes me weeks to throw a game with him. He's the worst player I've ever seen.

REBEL: Why throw the game?

JOURNEY: Ever since he had to leave Yale, he's needed a win.

(Rebel clicks on the computer.)

REBEL: I need another song in my head. Oh my Gawd. How much of this drum music you got?

JOURNEY: That music is sacred.

REBEL: There's a song here called "Powwow Mighty Mouse." You pray to Mighty Mouse?

JOURNEY: That's a kid's song. It's humor.

REBEL: Crazy Horse bullshit, bullshit.

JOURNEY: What are you doing?

REBEL: Going through his files.

JOURNEY: Get the fuck off Calvin's computer.

REBEL: My gawd.

JOURNEY: What?

REBEL: Why is Calvin contacting domestic terrorists?

EVAN: Please tell me you are kidding.

REBEL: All the usual suspects: Hutaree, ALF, Advanced White Society, Sovereign Citizens.

JOURNEY: I deleted those emails.

REBEL: I pulled up all his deleted files.

JOURNEY: You can do that?

EVAN: As I said, Rebel has an array of special training.

REBEL: Nigger-lynching idiots like this are the people we're trying to get away from, not be tied to.

JOURNEY: Sorry we're not the Klan poster-children you were hoping for.

EVAN: This is a problem, Journey. We need to see how deep this goes.

JOURNEY: Stop it!

(She grabs Calvin's laptop.)

REBEL: Give that back.

JOURNEY: It was me. I sent those emails. Not Calvin. He would flip if he knew.

REBEL: Give me the computer, girl. I'm not asking again.

JOURNEY: No.

(Rebel grabs a picture off the wall. He pulls it out of the glass and rips it apart.)

That's our mother!

(Rebel grabs a Native item off the wall and holds a knife to it.)

Grandpa made that.

REBEL: I will destroy everything you care about and burn this house to the ground if you don't start being a little more cooperative.

(Journey loosens her grip on the computer. Rebel grabs the computer from Journey. He and Evan read.)

EVAN: These are bad, hate-filled people, Journey.

JOURNEY: Says the head of the KKK.

REBEL: You wrote to ISIS? Are you an idiot?

JOURNEY: I told you, I've been mad. At Wounded Knee AIM took an armed stance against the government. People died on both sides and the world listened. Now Native people march and camp and pray and nothing happens. We are literally dying from our own health system and nothing happens.

EVAN: Just being in contact with some of these groups is against the law.

REBEL *(To Evan)*: We should get rid of her. Clean house and go.

JOURNEY: Wait, what?

EVAN: Let's think this out.

JOURNEY: Hey. Are you guys serious?

EVAN: You understand that Calvin is in custody with the federal government. If the NSA looks into his electronic history—

JOURNEY: I'll tell them it was me. Not Calvin.

EVAN: But it's his computer.

JOURNEY: He can't find out what I did.

EVAN: Well . . . we may be able to help. Rebel, can you get rid of the evidence on the computer?

REBEL: Yeah, sure. I can make it all go away.

JOURNEY: You can do that?

EVAN: There's even a possibility that our contact can get him out before they start digging too deep.

JOURNEY: I'll do whatever you want, if you got Calvin home safe. Put me in front of a camera now.

EVAN: It's a pretty big risk for us.

JOURNEY: This is bullshit. You claim you have all this power. I think it's a lie. You're just some scrawny white bitch—

(Rebel looks at her sharply.)

REBEL: She's about to be the first female Imperial Wizard of the Ku Klux Klan. A leader of thousands. And she has your life in her hands. Show some fucking respect.

EVAN: Even though things have become complicated, we should not lower ourselves to indecorous language.

REBEL: This bitch is asking for some fucking language.

EVAN: Perhaps. I'm going to the restroom. This way?

(Journey nods. Evan gets up and cringes as she goes.)

REBEL: You know, in another time and place, you'd be strung up in a tree with your boobs cut off by now.

JOURNEY: You wish.

REBEL: No. I don't. I really fucking don't. You can't even comprehend the evolution of thoughts that has gone on in the Klan. You can't ever understand that making it about killing each other off is us lowering ourselves to the level of animals. Evan Atwood has transformed my mind and the minds of thousands. I don't want you dead, Journey Good fucking Eagle. I want you to live your pathetic pagan, dirt-tent lives as free and pure as the day God put your ungrateful souls on this earth. I just want you to do it as far from me and my organization as possible. If that doesn't prove who's superior, then nothing fucking will.

(Journey studies Rebel.)

JOURNEY: You really believe that.

REBEL: I do.

JOURNEY: Know what I can't stand?

REBEL: I really don't.

JOURNEY: People who don't have the balls to follow through on what they believe in. Especially when it gets hard.

REBEL: Look, girl, I got balls.

JOURNEY: I thought you did.

REBEL: What's that mean?

JOURNEY: If you're gonna get rid of me, just do it. Don't be a pussy about it.

REBEL: Listen, girl, I was the bad-ass redneck. I grew up in the worst of the Southern Klan, such as it was. Went into the special fucking forces to stay out of prison. Sent straight to Afghanistan.

That's when I found out what fucked-up monsters people really are. Women . . . children. All that shit I saw

WHAT WOULD CRAZY HORSE DO?

. . . screwed me up good. When I got back, I heard Evan speak. I didn't know what the hell she was going on about, but I knew I didn't want no more of good ol' boys playing at something they don't understand. I talked to Evan that night, and she helped me see another path. A peaceful path. She showed me it wasn't the rag heads' fault they did the shit they did. She made me see them, and you, as God's creatures, fucked-up just the way he wanted them. She taught me to forgive, and for the first time in my life, hate fell away and I could see things clearly.

JOURNEY: I like my hate. It's the only thing keeping me going. Without my hate I'd be dead by now.

REBEL: I used to believe that, but think about it, if no one mixed with no one in the Middle East or in Germany or Japan we wouldn't have fought any of these fucking wars. All those people wouldn't be dead if everyone just kept to their own. The vision of Evan Atwood let me see that. It brought hope to my life.

JOURNEY: I'm so fucking happy for you.

REBEL: Look, girl, I'm trying to share something with you. Watch your tone.

JOURNEY: Or what? You'll rip up another picture? Tell me another story about your hope and enlightenment? Quote your fancy white cunt all you want but we both know you're just another piece of trailer trash, redneck dick that she would never fuck.

(Fast as a snake, Rebel grabs Journey's throat.)

REBEL: Shut your mouth.

JOURNEY: There he is. The true animal. White superiority my ass.

REBEL: I'm warning you, girl.

JOURNEY: There's nothing you can do to hurt me.

REBEL: You have no idea what I've done.

JOURNEY: You ever woke up from a blackout and found your boyfriend and his three best friends dead on the floor? Slipped on their blood, crawled through their piss and shit and brains to get to the guy you just had inside of you. Find him holding a gun in one hand and a lousy eight of clubs in the other. *(She laughs)* How fucked is that? Totally screwed over a lousy eight?

Neil watched his buddies shoot themselves one by one. He saw and smelled what I did, then still had the balls to pull the trigger all alone. I replay it in my head all the time. Even when I sleep. Especially when I sleep.

REBEL: You shouldn't do that.

JOURNEY: I couldn't let it go. At first . . . Calvin came home to take care of me. But lately I feel like seeing that, imagining what they did, makes me stronger. When I saw Grandpa's body crushed in the car and the drunk that hit him sleeping it off, I thought, "I can be as strong as Neil." So I hit that asshole over and over again as hard as I could. I felt his bones moving . . .

REBEL: Blood spraying . . .

JOURNEY: It felt so . . .

REBEL: Good.

JOURNEY: I would have killed him if Calvin hadn't come along.

REBEL: You know that's fucked-up, right?

JOURNEY: No shit.

REBEL: You really never been diagnosed?

JOURNEY: What the hell are you talking about?

REBEL: You've got all the signs of Post Traumatic Stress Disorder. Shit, screwed up as you are, you should be dead by now.

JOURNEY: I've got Calvin.

REBEL: But that hate you got, it's all out of whack cause of your PTSD.

JOURNEY: You don't know shit about me.

REBEL: I know you don't have control over how you feel. You do shit you don't understand and it's escalating. You're gonna cause some real pain soon, and the collateral damage is probably gonna be Calvin.

JOURNEY: I'd never hurt him.

REBEL: You're making the guy kill himself.

JOURNEY: He wants to too.

REBEL: Really? 'Cause the only person I've seen with a gun to their head tonight is you.

(Journey is confused.)

Look, you've got plenty to be pissed about, but, there's help out there to get you back in control. That's what you really want right?

JOURNEY: I don't know.

REBEL: I've been where you are and I'm telling you, there is another way out.

JOURNEY: Why do you care?

REBEL: Because your life can mean more than your death, Journey.

(It's that moment when everything you thought you knew, shifts.)

JOURNEY: I don't want to feel this way anymore.

REBEL: I know. Evan saved my life. She can save yours too.

JOURNEY: None of her Klan shit pertains to me.

REBEL: It's all about you. You and Calvin *are* the poster kids for racial separation. And Evan, she's national. She's got resources and funding you can't imagine. Once we announce, we'll be hounded by the press. And all that power and attention can be yours.

JOURNEY: For what?

REBEL: To mess up those that messed up your people. But legitimate like.

JOURNEY: I told you, I'm done marching and praying. I want change.

REBEL: So do we.

(Evan comes around the corner.)

EVAN: Arizona.

JOURNEY: What does that mean?

EVAN: Do you know that in Arizona it is now a crime to harbor an illegal immigrant? Voilà, automatic nonviolent separation of races.

JOURNEY: The Klan isn't going around passing anti-immigration laws in the middle of the desert.

EVAN: Free Americans is. It was a test case of our political lobby structure. Just a beginning, but a pretty effective start. While staying completely underground, we have influence over an entire state. Once we unveil our full potential . . . it's power you've never imagined. That power can be yours.

Who do you blame?

JOURNEY: The government.

REBEL: That's right.

EVAN: We're already working on the inside. Influencing elections, dismantling it from within.

Which agency pisses you off the most?

JOURNEY: Indian Health Services. People die every day from shit no one else in this country does.

EVAN: Let's expose them for exactly what they are. Then institute new policy to get better health care on reservations.

JOURNEY: It's not that easy.

EVAN: We start with this clinic right here. What do they need? Equipment? Staff? I can have things sent over next week.

JOURNEY: You're not serious.

EVAN: One call and I'll get you something they need. Not everything, but a good-faith start.

JOURNEY: There's no one to go to for depression and stuff.

REBEL: Maybe someone who does PTSD, like Dr. Rainey? Half this reservation probably has it.

EVAN: Good idea. He could set up the program then rotate his residents through, under his guidance. I'll send him an email now, letting him know we need to talk.

(Evan types.)

REBEL: He's good, Journey. Helped me with stuff.

EVAN: Done.

JOURNEY: An email doesn't mean you will make it happen.

EVAN: I've worked ten years to cut the cancer out of this organization. Once we launch Free Americans, I will have total support to do whatever I want.

REBEL: But taking over a clinic is big. Gonna need someone to run it.

EVAN: Calvin. He already knows the clinic, the Lakota people, the system. He would make a huge difference in changing it. It's too late to save the Marahotah, but the two of you can save other tribes.

JOURNEY: You really mean it.

EVAN: I do.

JOURNEY: The Marahotah dances and songs, they do have meaning.

EVAN: They changed my life and I've never even heard them.

JOURNEY: The old ways teach that if someone asks for the dances, they are being led by a spirit because they need healing. When Dr. Evans asked for the songs, Grandpa could not refuse. Nor would he want to. I think that's why Grandpa signed the contract with you.

EVAN: But if you believed in all that, you would not have refused.

JOURNEY: That was a mistake. I see that now.

EVAN: So if I ask you again, you will do the powwow?

JOURNEY: I have to. It's bigger than me. It's about our beliefs, our people.

EVAN: All those people will hear the songs. Be healed.

JOURNEY: Are you asking me for the songs, Evan?

EVAN: Yes.

JOURNEY: Then I'll do it.

EVAN: Really? Thank you, Journey.

JOURNEY: And you'll make the clinic happen?

EVAN: I will.

JOURNEY: But Calvin, he won't want to work with you.

EVAN: Doesn't he believe in the Marahotah traditions?

JOURNEY: He does but . . . he's different now.

EVAN: We will do whatever it takes to help him see we are sincere. You will get to see the doctor too. Get help.

JOURNEY: He'll like that.

REBEL: And his computer. I can permanently erase everything so no one can ever find it.

JOURNEY: You will do that? Make it so Calvin is safe?

REBEL: I'll need your router, boosters, external drives, everything.

JOURNEY: The router and stuff are in the back.

REBEL: Bring it here and we'll make this all go away. He'll never know what you did.

(Journey leaves the room.)

EVAN: I can't believe it. This powwow is going to happen.

REBEL: I'll take custody of the computer, in case we need to use it.

EVAN: No. Erase everything.

REBEL: I can erase the hard drives but the online history is out there for anyone to find.

EVAN: Can't you hide it or point it to someone else?

REBEL: Not completely.

EVAN: God used the Marahotah once before. I believe He sent Journey to us as a sign. Protecting them is protecting us.

REBEL: You really think she's a sign?

(Calvin bursts in. He looks for Journey.)

CALVIN: Journey. Where is my sister?

EVAN: She's fine. She's in the other room.

CALVIN: Journey!

JOURNEY *(From the other room)*: Calvin! Wait there.

CALVIN: What?

(He crosses toward her.)

REBEL: She said wait. How did you get out so fast?

CALVIN: I didn't do anything so they let me go.

REBEL *(To Evan)*: Or, they're using him.

(Rebel pats down Calvin.)

Did they take your clothes, shoes, jewelry? Give you anything as simple as a pen?

CALVIN: No. What the hell are you doing?

REBEL: Checking for bugs. You're clean.

CALVIN: Of course I am.

(He moves forward. Rebel gets in his way.)

REBEL: Did they ask about anything else?

CALVIN: Why would I answer to you?

REBEL: I want to be sure they don't know—

CALVIN: This is none of your business. I want to see my sister.
REBEL: She'll be back.

(Calvin pushes at Rebel, who stands firm.)

EVAN: Calvin, she's fine. Relax.
CALVIN: Journey!

(He pushes at Rebel again. It's like a wall.)

REBEL: I don't want to do this, Calvin.
CALVIN: Get the hell out of my way!

(It turns into a scuffle. Rebel quickly flips Calvin and has him on the floor.)

REBEL: Settle down now, boy.
CALVIN: Journey!

(Journey runs in with a duffel bag.)

JOURNEY: Calvin! I'm fine. It's OK.
CALVIN *(To Rebel)*: Get off me.
JOURNEY: Rebel's trying to help.
CALVIN: What has happened here?
JOURNEY: It's gonna be OK. We have a plan now. Just like you wanted.
REBEL: You OK, son?

(Calvin gets up, grabs Journey, and pulls her away from Evan and Rebel.)

CALVIN: I want you out of our house. I don't give a shit about the contract or Journey shooting you or whatever. Get out!

JOURNEY: Calvin, wait. You trust me, right?

(Calvin hesitates a little too long, torn.)

You don't trust me? Me? I'm your twin.

CALVIN: I trust you with my life. I just . . . lately . . . you know.

JOURNEY: They know about me and the drunk driver . . . everything.

CALVIN: You told them that? Then no, I don't trust you. But I know how to help you. Both of us.

REBEL: We're gonna get her the help she needs.

CALVIN: *We?*

EVAN: Calvin, we're going to start a mental-health program at your IHS clinic.

CALVIN: What?

EVAN: To show our good faith and support of you and Journey. We'd like you to oversee the program. You can work right here on the reservation.

CALVIN: You expect me to believe that in the last few hours the KKK has taken an interest in mental health on this reservation? To be nice and give me a job? I'm not an idiot. What the hell is going on?

JOURNEY: Calvin, it's hard to explain, but this is what Grandpa wanted, a way to help others through the Marahotah ways. This is more than a plan. It's a purpose.

CALVIN: It's not.

JOURNEY: Just listen to them.

REBEL: I know what she's going through. We can help her—

CALVIN: She's going through your brainwash bullshit. If you won't leave, we will.

(Calvin grabs Journey and pulls her toward the door. Journey resists. They struggle.)

JOURNEY: No. We can't go.   CALVIN: I'm trying to save you!
   They're helping you!   Stop fighting me!
   Let me go!

(*It turns bad, desperate. Journey freaks and lashes out at Calvin. He fights to control her.*)

JOURNEY: You're hurting me!

(*Rebel steps in and breaks Journey free from Calvin. Journey stays with Rebel, shaken. The three face off against Calvin.*)

REBEL: I don't care if she's your sister, don't lay a hand on her again.

CALVIN: Are you fucking kidding me? Journey. Journey?

JOURNEY: You hurt me!

CALVIN: I'm sorry I scared you.

JOURNEY: We will bring the Marahotah ways back to the world. We can save people. Evan will help us do that.

CALVIN: They've taken you away from me.

JOURNEY: You left me first.

CALVIN: You told me and Rebel to go.

JOURNEY: Not tonight.

CALVIN: It was Yale. And I gave it all up for you.

JOURNEY: Long before that. I know you never believed in the twin pact. For years I thought I could convince you, but now—

CALVIN: You're right. I was stalling all these years. Trying to keep you alive. But tonight I finally figured it out. When the agents were taking me out of the clinic, all I could think of was you and your stupid meme. So I yell, "This is what Crazy Horse would do!" and for the first time in my life I fight. The Indians all cheered and I felt fucking great as they wrestled me into the car.

Then this huge fed looks me straight in the eye and says, "Who the fuck is Crazy Horse?" It was like he grabbed my heart with his fist. Then the guy leans in and says, "Is Crazy Horse the ring leader?" I said, "He's the greatest Lakota war chief in history. He defeated Custer. They're carving the world's largest monument in his honor." He says, "Too bad, could have cut yourself a deal."

I rode alone in the back of that car and shit got simple. Everything in my life has been focused on meaning something to the world and I thought you screwed it up by going crazy and making me quit school. But in that car I realized we've been fighting all our lives against an enemy that doesn't even know we exist. We've already been mowed down and forgotten. We're mulch.

JOURNEY: I know.

CALVIN: I swore if I ever got back to you, I'd never let you go again. We do it tonight. On our terms, together forever.

(They cling to each other fiercely.)

JOURNEY: I love you, Calvin.

CALVIN: I love you so much.

JOURNEY: But I was wrong. Our lives can make a difference.

CALVIN: Nothing we do matters.

JOURNEY: We have a plan.

CALVIN: What about *our* plan?

JOURNEY: In the end, even Crazy Horse went to the fort.

CALVIN: And his own people killed him.

JOURNEY: Hoka hey, sweet brother.

(Journey pulls away. Calvin sees the truth and his heart breaks. He grabs the gun.
Blackout. Gunshot.)

SCENE FIVE

The powwow. We hear drums warming up.

EVAN *(Voice-over):* There is a sickness in our nation. Our race. Our organization. We cannot be truly proud, truly strong, truly free until all of God's creation is empowered to fulfill the separate destinies that God intends for each of them.

We begin the healing by welcoming into our circle the first American Indian Chapter of Free Americans. The lessons from the genocide of the Native American people are the lessons that will prevent the genocide of us all.

Strength in purity.

(Lights up on Journey dressed in new regalia for the powwow. She opens her dance shawl, revealing the KKK logo designed within the four directions. The shawl whirls as Journey spins into a Native dance. She seems to float above the earth, timeless and free.)

END OF PLAY

LARISSA FASTHORSE (Sicangu Lakota) is an award-winning playwright, director, and choreographer. She is the co-founder of Indigenous Direction, the nation's leading consulting company for Indigenous arts and audiences, which recently produced the first land acknowledgment on national television for the Macy's Thanksgiving Day Parade on NBC.

With *The Thanksgiving Play*, Larissa is the first Native American playwright in the history of American theater to have a top ten most-produced play.

She created a trilogy of community-engaged plays with Cornerstone Theater Company: *Urban Rez*; *Native Nation*, the largest Indigenous theater prodution in the history of American theater with more than four hundred artists; and *The L/D/Nakota Project* (set in Larissa's hometown of South Dakota). Other plays include *Landless and Cow Pie Bingo*, *Average Family*, *Teaching Disco Squaredancing to Our Elders: A Class Presentation*, *Vanishing Point*, and *Cherokee Family Reunion*.

Theatres that have commissioned or developed plays with Larissa include The Public Theater, Yale Repertory Theatre, the Guthrie Theater, History Theatre, the Kennedy Center Theater for Young Audiences, Baltimore Center Stage, Seattle Rep, Arizona Theatre Company, Mixed Blood Theatre, Perseverance Theatre, The Lark Playwrights' Week, Milwaukee Repertory Theater, Center Theatre Group's L.A. Writers' Workshop, and The Ground Floor at Berkeley Repertory Theatre.

She is currently in development as the creator for projects with Disney, NBC, and DreamWorks.

Awards include a 2020 MacArthur Fellowship, the PEN USA Literary Award for Drama, the NEA Distinguished New Play Development Grant, the Joe Dowling Annamaghkerrig Fellowship, the AATE Distinguished Play Award, an Inge Residency, a Sundance/Ford Foundation Fellowship, the Aurand Harris Fellowship, the UCLA Native American Program Woman of the Year, and numerous Ford, Mellon, and NEA grants. She is a current member of the Playwright's Union, Director's Lab West 2015, Playwright's Center Core Writers, and she is a board member of Playwrights Horizons.

Larissa lives in Santa Monica with her husband, the sculptor Edd Hogan.

*Theatre Communications Group would like to offer
our special thanks to Stephanie Ansin and Spencer Stewart
for their generous support of the publication of*
The Thanksgiving Play/What Would Crazy
Horse Do? *by Larissa FastHorse*

THEATRE COMMUNICATIONS GROUP's mission is to lead for a just and thriving theatre ecology. Through its Core Values of Activism, Artistry, Diversity, and Global Citizenship, TCG advances a better world for theatre and a better world because of theatre. TCG Books is the largest independent trade publisher of dramatic literature in North America, with 18 Pulitzer Prizes for Best Play on its book list. The book program commits to the life-long career of its playwrights, keeping all of their plays in print. TCG Books' other authors include: Annie Baker, Nilo Cruz, Jackie Sibblies Drury, Athol Fugard, Quiara Alegría Hudes, David Henry Hwang, Branden Jacobs-Jenkins, The Kilroys, Tony Kushner, Young Jean Lee, Tracy Letts, Lynn Nottage, Jeremy O'Harris, Dael Orlandersmith, Suzan-Lori Parks, Sarah Ruhl, Stephen Sondheim, Paula Vogel, Anne Washburn, and August Wilson, among many others.

Support TCG's work in the theatre field by becoming a member or donor: www.tcg.org